MacBook A

The Complete Step-by-St
Features and Functions o ... with
M2 Chip Designed for Beginners and Seniors

Curtis

Campbell

Disclaimer

The information in this book is based on personal experience and anecdotal evidence. Although the author has made every attempt to achieve an accuracy of the information gathered in this book, they make no representation or warranties concerning the accuracy or completeness of the contents of this book. Your circumstances may not be suited to some illustrations in this book.

The author disclaims any liability arising directly or indirectly from the use of this book. Readers are encouraged to seek Medical. Accounting, legal, or professional help when required.

This guide is for informational purposes only, and the author does not accept any responsibilities for any liabilities resulting from the use of this information. While every attempt has been made to verify the information provided here, the author cannot assume any responsibility for errors, inaccuracies or omission.

Printed in the United States of America

Table of Contents

INTRODUCTION

This guide is crafted for individuals who have recently welcomed the MacBook Air 2023 into their lives or considering making it their digital partner. We'll walk you through every step, ensuring you grasp the basics and advance to harness its potential fully.

Get ready to be captivated by the elegance, simplicity, and boundless potential of the MacBook Air 2023. Let's get in together and uncover the technology that awaits your fingertips!

CHAPTER ONE

MacBook Air 2023 Unique Features

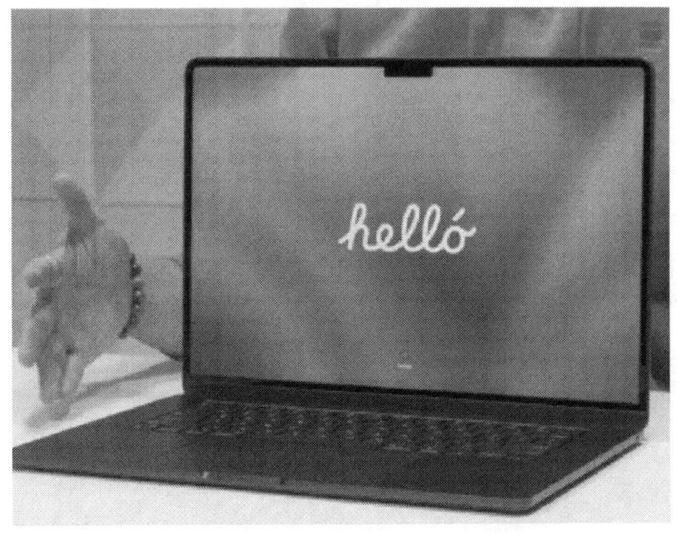

Here's a comprehensive guide that unveils the remarkable features of Apple's latest creation: the world's thinnest 15.3-inch MacBook Air, unveiled at WWDC 2023. From its sleek design to its impressive performance, you're about to uncover its technological excellence.

A Visual Masterpiece with Liquid Retina Display

Step into a world of visual brilliance with the MacBook Air's stunning 15.3-inch Liquid Retina display. Immerse yourself in the vibrant spectrum of 1 billion colors, creating visuals that burst with life and clarity. With a remarkable brightness of up to 500 nits, your screen becomes a canvas of vividness, ensuring every detail shines through. Whether editing photos, watching movies, or working on projects, the Liquid Retina display transforms your experience into a visual symphony.

Power and Performance, Redefined

Behind the scenes, the MacBook Air 2023 houses a processor powerhouse that propels your tasks to new heights. Say goodbye to slowdowns and hello to seamless multitasking. This laptop boasts an impressive battery life of up to 18 hours – a staggering 50 percent more than its PC counterparts. Even with the display at its peak brilliance, you're assured of unwavering performance throughout your day. Whether you're working on intensive projects or streaming your favorite content, the MacBook Air rises to the occasion.

Elegance Meets Portability

The MacBook Air's sleek and slim design, measuring a mere 11.5mm, redefines what it means to be portable. Weighing just 3.3 pounds, it's your ideal companion for work and play, effortlessly slipping into your bag without weighing you down. Despite its slender frame, this laptop stands strong, ensuring durability that withstands the test of time. It's a testament to Apple's engineering prowess that the MacBook Air is nearly 40 percent thinner and half a pound lighter than its PC counterparts, making it a true marvel of modern technology.

Enhanced Multimedia Experience

Indulge your senses with the MacBook Air's six-speaker sound system, delivering immersive audio that surrounds you. Whether enjoying music, watching videos, or joining virtual meetings, the MacBook Air ensures crystal-clear sound that elevates your experience. Capture life's moments with stunning clarity using the high-quality camera, adding a new dimension to your video calls and content creation.

A Comparative Advantage

Apple's dedication to innovation is evident as the MacBook Air 2023 outshines its PC competition. With double the resolution and a 25 percent increase in brightness, the MacBook Air's display experience is in a league of its own. Its compact design, measuring only 11.5mm, makes it the world's thinnest 15-inch laptop, a testament to engineering brilliance. Its featherlight weight of 3.3 pounds ensures effortless portability without compromising on durability.

The 15.3-inch MacBook Air 2023 is more than just a laptop; it's a technological masterpiece that fuses elegance, performance, and innovation. With a display that mesmerizes, a power that astounds and a captivating design, this laptop redefines what it means to be at the forefront of technology. Experience the future with the MacBook Air and elevate your journey into endless possibilities.

Getting Started Checklists

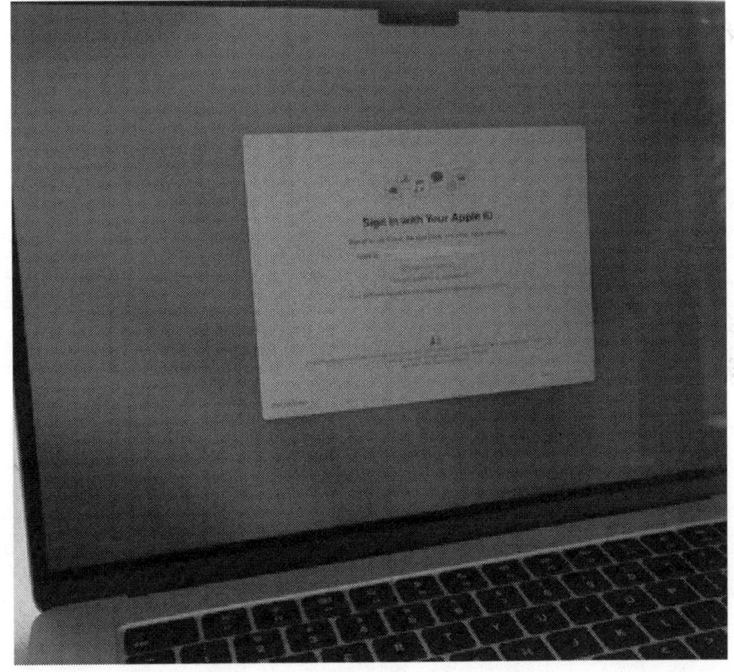

This guide will walk you through the essential steps to set up and configure your MacBook Air 2023, ensuring a smooth and hassle-free experience.

Step 1: Unboxing and Initial Setup

Carefully unbox your MacBook Air 2023, removing all packaging materials.

Open the lid of your MacBook Air to power it on.

Select your language and region preferences when prompted.

Connect to a Wi-Fi network by selecting your network and entering the password.

Step 2: Apple ID and iCloud Setup

Sign in with your existing Apple ID or create a new one if you don't have an account.

Choose whether to use iCloud for syncing your data across devices, and select the apps you want to use with iCloud.

Step 3: Data Migration (Optional)

You can transfer your data during setup if you're migrating from an old Mac or PC.

Use the "Migration Assistant" to transfer files, apps, and settings from your previous device.

Follow the on-screen instructions to complete the migration process.

Step 4: System Updates

Check for and install any available macOS updates to ensure your MacBook Air runs the latest software.

Go to the Apple menu (□) > "System Preferences" > "Software Update" to check for updates.

Step 5: Privacy and Security

Navigate to the Apple menu (□) > "System Preferences" > "Security & Privacy."

Review and adjust your privacy settings, such as location services, app permissions, and firewall settings.

Step 6: Personalization

Customize your MacBook Air by setting your preferred display resolution, desktop wallpaper, and screen saver.

Add your favorite apps to the Dock for quick access.

Step 7: Internet Browsers and Apps

Open the App Store and download your preferred internet browser (e.g., Safari, Chrome, Firefox).

Install essential apps from the App Store, such as messaging apps, office suites, and media players.

Step 8: Time Machine Backup (Recommended)

Connect an external hard drive and set up Time Machine for automatic backups.

Go to the Apple menu (□) > "System Preferences" > "Time Machine" to configure backup settings.

Step 9: Keyboard and Trackpad Settings

Customize keyboard shortcuts and trackpad gestures according to your preferences.

Navigate to the Apple menu (□) > "System Preferences" > "Keyboard" and "Trackpad" to make adjustments.

Step 10: User Accounts (Optional)

If you're sharing your MacBook Air, create separate user accounts for each user.

Go to the Apple menu (□) > "System Preferences" > "Users & Groups" to manage user accounts.

Recommended Accessories

Consider adding valuable accessories to enhance your experience and make the most of your new tech companion.

Step 1: Protective Case or Sleeve

Invest in a high-quality protective case or sleeve to safeguard your MacBook Air from scratches, dings, and dust when not in use or during transport. Look for a slim, durable option that fits your style.

Step 2: External Storage

Consider getting an external SSD or HDD to expand your storage capacity; this is particularly useful for storing large files, photos, videos, and backups. Ensure it's compatible with USB-C or Thunderbolt 3 for faster data transfer speeds.

Step 3: USB-C Hub or Dock

Since the MacBook Air has limited USB-C ports, a USB-C hub or dock is invaluable for connecting various peripherals simultaneously. For versatility, look for one with multiple USB ports, HDMI, SD card reader, and Ethernet.

Step 4: Bluetooth Mouse and Keyboard

Enhance your productivity with a wireless Bluetooth mouse and keyboard. Choose ergonomic designs for comfortable use during long work sessions.

Step 5: External Monitor

Boost your multitasking capabilities with an external monitor. This accessory is ideal for extending your display or working on larger projects. Ensure compatibility with your MacBook Air's video output.

Step 6: Headphones or Earbuds

Invest in good headphones or earbuds for immersive sound quality and to keep your workspace quiet. Look for options with noise-canceling features for enhanced focus.

Step 7: Laptop Stand or Cooling Pad

Elevate your MacBook Air for better ergonomics by using a laptop stand; this helps reduce strain on your neck and wrists. A cooling pad can also help maintain optimal temperature during intensive tasks.

Step 8: Webcam Cover

Protect your privacy using a webcam cover that can be easily attached to your MacBook Air's built-in webcam; this ensures your camera remains covered when not in use.

Step 9: Portable Charger/Power Bank

Stay powered up on the go with a portable charger or power bank. Look for a model with USB-C charging to keep your MacBook Air and other devices charged while traveling.

Step 10: Cable Management Solutions

Keep your workspace tidy with cable management accessories like cable clips, organizers, and sleeves. These tools help prevent cable clutter and make your setup more organized.

Note: It's advisable to research and ensure the compatibility of each accessory with your MacBook Air 2023 before making a purchase.

Connectivity Options

The latest 15-inch MacBook Air released in 2023 boasts an array of multipurpose ports, including a pair of Thunderbolt connectors, a MagSafe attachment, and a dedicated headphone jack.

These dual Thunderbolt/USB 4 ports have been designed to facilitate rapid data transfers, reaching remarkable speeds of up to 40Gbps. Furthermore, they offer the added convenience of expeditious charging for the MacBook Air. The headphone jack is primed to accommodate high-impedance headphones, ensuring an enhanced audio experience.

Significant enhancements are evident in the upgraded 1080p webcam, now powered by the advanced M2 image signal processor. This enhancement results in sharp and detailed image quality, lending a new dimension to video interactions. Notably, Center Stage is omitted; Apple has ingeniously introduced an innovative feature within macOS Ventura. This feature seamlessly integrates the iPhone camera with the Mac, enabling it to function as a webcam – a dynamic solution for improved video conferencing and content creation.

Tips for Maintenance

Maintaining your MacBook Air 2023 longevity and optimal performance is essential to ensure a smooth and efficient user experience.

Tip 1: Keep it Clean

Regularly clean the exterior and screen of your MacBook Air using a soft, lint-free cloth. Avoid using abrasive materials that could scratch the surface. Gently wipe away smudges, dust, and fingerprints to maintain its appearance.

Tip 2: Proper Storage

Store your MacBook Air in a clean, dry environment when not in use. Avoid exposing it to extreme temperatures, direct sunlight, or humidity, as these factors can negatively impact its internal components.

Tip 3: Update Software

Keep your MacBook Air's operating system and apps up to date. Regular software updates often include critical bug fixes, security enhancements, and performance optimizations, contributing to a smoother user experience.

Tip 4: Manage Storage

Regularly review your storage usage and remove unnecessary files and applications. Use the built-in "Storage Management" tool to identify and clear space, ensuring your MacBook Air operates efficiently.

Tip 5: Backup Data

Set up automatic backups using Time Machine to safeguard your important data. In case of unforeseen issues, you can restore your MacBook Air 2023 to its previous state without losing valuable information.

Tip 6: Temperature Control

Avoid using your MacBook Air on soft surfaces like beds or sofas, as these can obstruct airflow and lead to overheating. Use a hard, flat surface or a cooling pad to ensure proper ventilation.

Tip 7: App Management

Close unused apps to free up system resources; running too many applications (simultaneously) can strain your MacBook Air's performance and battery life.

Tip 8: Battery Care

Maintain your battery's health by avoiding extreme heat and deep discharges. Occasionally calibrate the battery by fully charging and then fully discharging it to help ensure accurate battery life readings.

Tip 9: Secure Internet Practices

Use reputable antivirus and security software to protect your MacBook Air from malware and online threats. Be cautious when downloading files or clicking on links from unknown sources.

Tip 10: Professional Servicing

If you encounter persistent performance issues or hardware problems, seek professional assistance.

Apple-certified technicians can diagnose and resolve issues to ensure your MacBook Air's optimal functioning.

CHAPTER TWO

Dock Location

The Dock is a fundamental feature of macOS that provides quick access to your most-used applications, files, and functions since you're new to using the MacBook Air 2023, learning how to locate and utilize the Dock is essential for a smooth and efficient computing experience.

By the end of this guide, you can confidently locate the Dock on your MacBook Air and understand its default position for easy access to frequently used applications.

Step 1.1: Look at the Bottom of the Screen

The Dock is usually at the bottom of your MacBook Air's screen by default.

Look at the bottom edge of your screen to see if you can spot the Dock.

Step 1.2: Recognizing the Dock Icons

The Dock contains icons representing applications, folders, and files.

Icons for frequently used apps may already be present in the Dock.

These icons are shortcuts that allow you to open the corresponding applications or files with a single click.

Step 1.3: Dock Position Options

While the default position is at the bottom, you can move the Dock to other screen parts.

To explore Dock position options, go to "System Preferences" from the Apple menu (□) in the top-left corner of your screen.

Click "Dock & Menu Bar" to access settings for customizing the Dock's position and behavior.

Step 1.4: Auto-Hide Feature

macOS offers an "Auto-Hide" feature that allows the Dock to disappear when you're not using it, giving you more screen space.

To turn Auto-Hide on or off, go to "System Preferences" > "Dock & Menu Bar" and check/uncheck the "Automatically hide and show the Dock" option.

Step 1.5: Keyboard Shortcut to Reveal the Dock

You can quickly reveal the Dock by moving your cursor to the screen's bottom edge or pressing your keyboard's "Control" and "F3" keys.

Dock Appearance

Step 1: Icons and Application Shortcuts

The icons in the Dock represent your frequently used applications. To add an app to the Dock, follow these simple steps:

Locate the desired app in the "Applications" folder or use Spotlight Search (press Command + Space and start typing the app's name).

Click and drag the app icon from the Applications folder or Search results onto the Dock.

Release the mouse button to drop the icon onto the Dock, and it will be added as a shortcut.

Step 2: Rearranging Icons

Organizing the icons in your Dock is easy:

Click and hold the icon you want to move.

Drag it to the desired position within the Dock.

Release the mouse button to place the icon in its new position.

Step 3: Adjusting Dock Size

You can resize the Dock for optimal viewing:

Click anywhere on the Dock's background.

A contextual menu will appear. Hover over "Dock Preferences" and click on it.

In the Dock Preferences window, you'll find a slider labeled "Size." Drag the slider left or right to adjust the Dock's size.

Observe the Dock as it changes size in real-time. Release the slider when you're satisfied with the size.

Step 4: Magnification Options

Magnification makes icons larger when you hover over them:

In the same Dock Preferences window, check the box labeled "Magnification."

Use the slider next to "Magnification" to adjust the degree of magnification.

Hover your cursor over an icon in the Dock to see the magnified effect.

Tips:

Be mindful of the Dock's size and magnification settings to ensure a comfortable viewing experience.

Experiment with the Dock's layout to optimize efficiency and aesthetics.

Adding and Removing Apps

Step 1: Adding Apps to the Dock

Adding apps to the Dock is a straightforward process that requires just a few simple steps:

Locate the App: Open the "Applications" folder on your MacBook Air. You can access this folder by clicking the "Finder" icon in the Dock and selecting "Applications" from the sidebar.

Drag and Drop: Find the app you want to add to the Dock. Click on the app's icon, then drag it to the Dock.

Arrange the App: Once the app's icon is on the Dock, you can arrange its position by dragging it left or right; this allows you to prioritize the apps you use most frequently.

Step 2: Removing Apps from the Dock

Cleaning up your Dock by removing unwanted apps is just as easy:

Locate the App on the Dock: Find the app you want to withdraw from the Dock. Its icon will indicate it.

Remove with Right-Click: Right-click (or control-click) on the app's icon. A contextual menu will appear.

Choose "Remove from Dock": From the contextual menu, hover over the "Options" submenu, then select "Remove from Dock."

Folders in the Dock

Step 1: Understanding the Concept of Dock Folders:

Dock folders allow you to group related apps and files for easy access. Think of them as virtual containers that help you maintain a well-organized Dock.

Step 2: Creating a New Folder in the Dock:

Locate your Dock at the bottom of the screen.

Find a space on the Dock.

Control-click (right-click) on the area.

From the context menu, hover over "Folder" and select "New Folder."

A new folder will appear on your Dock, ready to be customized.

Step 3: Renaming and Customizing Folders:

Click on the newly created folder to select it.

Press the "Return" key on your keyboard to activate the renaming mode.

Type in the desired name for your folder (e.g., "Productivity Apps").

Drag and drop app icons or files into the folder to add them.

Step 4: Opening Applications from Dock Folders:

Click on the folder in the Dock to open it.

Inside the folder, click on the app icon you want to use.

The selected app will launch, allowing you to start working or exploring.

Step 5: Removing Apps from Dock Folders:

Open the folder containing the app you want to remove.

Click and drag the app icon out of the folder.

Once the icon is outside the folder, release the mouse button to remove the app from the folder.

Step 6: Rearranging and Deleting Dock Folders:

Click and hold the folder you want to rearrange.

Drag the folder to your desired position on the Dock.

To delete a folder, drag it out of the Dock until you see the "Remove" label, then release the mouse button.

Tips and Tricks:

Customize folder icons: Control-click the folder, select "Show in Finder," and then paste an image onto the folder icon in Finder's Get Info window.

Utilize subfolders: Create nested folders within main folders for even more organization.

Use the "Keep in Dock" option: Control-click an app, hover over "Options," and select "Keep in Dock" to quickly add apps to your Dock.

Document Shortcuts

Step 1: Locating Your Document

Open the Finder by clicking the smiling face icon in the Dock or pressing "Command + N" on your keyboard.

Navigate to the folder where your desired document is located.

Step 2: Creating a Document Shortcut

Locate the document you want to create a shortcut for.

Click and hold the document icon.

While holding the icon, drag it down to the Dock area.

Position the document icon where you want the shortcut to appear in the Dock.

Release the mouse button to drop the shortcut onto the Dock.

Step 3: Customizing Document Shortcut Appearance

Control-click (right-click) the document shortcut in the Dock.

Hover over "Options" in the context menu.

Select "Show in Finder" to quickly locate the document's original location.

To change the shortcut's name, control-click it, select "Rename," and type in the new name.

Step 4: Removing Document Shortcuts

Locate the document shortcut you wish to remove in the Dock.

Click and drag the shortcut icon upwards, away from the Dock.

Release the mouse button to remove the shortcut from the Dock.

Step 5: Organizing Document Shortcuts

Arrange your document shortcuts by clicking and dragging them within the Dock.

Drop the shortcuts in your preferred order to create an organized layout.

Consider using folders within the Dock (as described in a previous guide) to further categorize and manage your document shortcuts.

Tips and Tricks

- Keep important documents at your fingertips: Add frequently used files like reports, presentations, and spreadsheets to the Dock for swift access.
- Utilize smart folders: Create folders to automatically collect and display specific types of documents in one place.
- Update shortcuts as needed: If you move or rename a document, don't forget to update its shortcut accordingly.

Recent Apps and Documents

Step 1: Locating the "Recent" Section

Look at the right side of your Dock, where you'll find the "Recent" section.

The "Recent" section displays icons of your most recently used apps and documents.

Step 2: Accessing Recent Apps

Click on the "Recent" section in the Dock.

A menu will appear, showcasing the icons of your recently used apps.

Click on an app icon to quickly launch the respective application.

Step 3: Accessing Recent Documents

Click on the "Recent" section in the Dock again.

This time, the menu will display icons of your recently opened documents.

Hover over a document icon to reveal its full name and path.

Click on a document icon to open it with the associated application.

Step 4: Clearing Recent Items

Now, control-click (right-click) on an app or document icon within the "Recent" section.

From the context menu, select "Clear" to remove that specific item from the list.

To clear all recent items, control-click any app or document icon and choose "Clear Recent."

Step 5: Customizing "Recent" Preferences

Click on the Apple menu () in the top-left corner of the screen.

Select "System Preferences" from the dropdown menu.

Choose "Dock & Menu Bar."

In the "Recent items" section, adjust the number of apps and documents displayed in the "Dock" section.

Tips and Tricks

- Stay organized: Use the "Recent" section to resume work on files you were recently using quickly.
- Privacy and security: If you're concerned about privacy, consider adjusting the settings to limit the number of recent items displayed.
- Clear selectively: Clear individual items from the "Recent" section to remove clutter while keeping essential things accessible.

Running Apps Indicator

Step 1: Identifying Running Apps in the Dock

Open applications appear in the Dock with a subtle indicator.

An illuminated dot below the app icon signifies that the app is currently running.

Step 2: Switching Between Running Apps

Click on a running app's icon in the Dock to bring it to the forefront.

If you want to switch to a different running app, click on its icon in the Dock.

The previously active app will be hidden in the background.

Step 3: Managing Running Apps

Minimize an app's window by clicking the yellow button in the top-left corner.

To hide an app without minimizing, press "Command + H" while the app is active.

Use "Mission Control" (three-finger swipe up or "Control + Up Arrow" key) to view all open app windows and spaces.

Step 4: Quitting Running Apps

Right-click (Control-click) on the app's icon in the Dock.

From the context menu, select "Quit" to close the app.

Alternatively, press "Command + Q" while the app is active to quit it.

Step 5: Force Quitting Apps

If an app becomes unresponsive, press "Option + Command + Esc" simultaneously.

A window will appear showing a list of currently running apps.

Select the unresponsive app and click "Force Quit."

Step 6: Managing Apps with Mission Control

Launch Mission Control (three-finger swipe up or press "Control + Up Arrow").

Move the cursor to the top of the screen to reveal app windows and spaces.

Drag app windows to different spaces or click on a window to make it active.

Tips and Tricks

- Use keyboard shortcuts: Press "Command + Tab" to cycle through running apps quickly.
- Keep your Dock tidy: Remove unused apps from the Dock to focus on your most important tasks.
- Customize your Dock: Control-click the Dock's separator line and adjust settings like magnification and position.

Minimizing Windows to the Dock

Step 1: Open and Arrange Your Windows

Open the applications and windows you want to work with.

Arrange the windows on your screen as needed for your tasks.

Step 2: Minimizing a Window to the Dock

Locate the window you want to minimize.

Click the window's yellow button (usually in the top-left corner).

The window will shrink and be minimized to the right side of the Dock.

Step 3: Restoring a Minimized Window

Look at the right side of the Dock, where minimized windows are displayed.

Click on the minimized window's icon to restore it to its previous size and position.

Step 4: Minimize Multiple Windows

If multiple windows are open in an application, click the yellow button on one of them to minimize it.

All windows from that application will be minimized to the same icon on the Dock.

Click the minimized icon to view and restore individual windows.

Step 5: Organizing Minimized Windows

Drag and drop minimized window icons within the Dock to arrange their order.

Place minimized windows next to each other for easy access.

Step 6: Clearing Minimized Windows

Control-click (right-click) on a minimized window icon in the Dock.

Select "Close Window" from the context menu to remove the minimized window.

To clear all minimized windows, control-click on any minimized icon and choose "Close All Windows."

Tips and Tricks

- Use keyboard shortcuts: Press "Command + M" to minimize the active window to the Dock.
- Customize window behavior: Adjust the "Minimize windows using" setting in System Preferences > Dock to choose between minimizing the Dock or the application's icon.

- Stay organized: Regularly review minimized windows to ensure you're not cluttering your workspace.

Using Stacks

Step 1: Understanding Stacks in the Dock

Stacks are a feature that automatically organizes files on the Dock.

Files within a Stack are grouped based on file type or sorting criteria.

Step 2: Enabling Stacks

Right-click (Control-click) on a space on the Dock.

Hover over "Folder" and choose "Use Stacks."

Step 3: Organizing Files into Stacks

Drag files from your desktop or Finder into the Dock.

Drop the files onto the Stack area of the Dock.

Stacks will automatically group files by type (e.g., documents, images, downloads).

Step 4: Accessing Stacks

Click on a Stack icon in the Dock to reveal its contents.

The Stack will expand, displaying the grouped files.

Click again to collapse the Stack and reduce clutter.

Step 5: Customizing Stacks

Control-click (right-click) on a Stack icon in the Dock.

Choose "List," "Grid," or "Automatic" to change the Stack's display style.

"Automatic" intelligently selects the best view based on the number of files in the Stack.

Step 6: Navigating within Stacks

Click on a file within a Stack to open it with the associated application.

Use arrow keys to navigate through the Stack's contents.

Tips and Tricks

- Use Downloads Stack: Enable the Downloads Stack to organize your downloaded files automatically.
- Stack by Kind: For a more specific grouping, organize files within a Stack by kind (e.g., PDFs, images).
- Keep Dock organized: Regularly review and manage your Stacks to maintain a clutter-free Dock.

Hidden Apps and Auto-Hide

Step 1: Hiding Apps from the Dock

Locate the app you want to hide in the Dock.

Now, control-click (right-click) on the app's icon.

From the context menu, hover over "Options."

Select "Remove from Dock" to hide the app.

Step 2: Enabling Auto-Hide for the Dock

Click on the Apple menu () in the top-left corner of the screen.

Choose "System Preferences" from the dropdown menu.

Select "Dock & Menu Bar."

Check the box next to "Automatically hide and show the Dock."

Step 3: Using Auto-Hide for More Space

With auto-hide enabled, move your cursor to the bottom of the screen.

The Dock will slide out, revealing your apps.

Move your cursor away from the Dock to hide it again.

Step 4: Bringing Hidden Dock Back

Move your cursor to the bottom of the screen when you want to access the Dock.

The Dock will slide out, revealing your hidden apps.

Click on an app icon to open it.

Step 5: Customizing Auto-Hide Behavior

In "Dock & Menu Bar" preferences, adjust the "Size" slider to control the Dock's size when visible.

Use the "Position on screen" dropdown to choose where the Dock appears when visible.

Tips and Tricks

- Utilize keyboard shortcuts: Press "Command + Option + D" to toggle Dock visibility.
- Use auto-hide strategically: If you have a small screen, auto-hide can provide more space for your applications.
- Keep essentials visible: Leave frequently used apps visible on the Dock even with auto-hide enabled.

Dock Preferences

Step 1: Accessing Dock Preferences

Click on the Apple menu () in the top-left corner of the screen.

Choose "System Preferences" from the dropdown menu.

Select "Dock & Menu Bar."

Step 2: Customizing Appearance

Adjust the "Size" slider to control the size of the Dock icons when visible.

Choose the "Position on screen" dropdown to select where the Dock appears (bottom, left, right).

Step 3: Enabling and Customizing Magnification

Check the box next to "Magnification" to enable icon magnification.

Drag the "Magnification" slider to adjust the level of magnification.

When you move the cursor over Dock icons, they will magnify for easier visibility.

Step 4: Animating Opening Applications

Check the box next to "Animate opening applications" to enable the animation effect.

When you click on an application in the Dock, it will visually expand as it opens.

Step 5: Enabling Auto-Hide

Check the box next to "Automatically hide and show the Dock" to enable auto-hide.

The Dock will slide out when you move the cursor to its location and hide when you move it away.

Step 6: Minimize Using

Choose either "Genie effect" or "Scale effect" from the "Minimize using" dropdown.

This setting determines the animation style when you minimize windows.

Step 7: Double-Click a Window's Title Bar

Choose between "Minimize" or "Maximize" from the dropdown.

When you double-click a window's title bar, it will perform the selected action.

Step 8: Prefer Tabs When Opening Documents

Choose "Always" or "In Full Screen Only" from the dropdown.

This setting controls how new document windows are opened in applications that support tabs.

Step 9: Show Recent Applications in Dock

Check the box next to "Show recent applications in Dock" to display recently used apps.

Step 10: Show Indicators for Open Applications

Check the box next to "Show indicators for open applications" to display a light indicator below open app icons.

Step 11: Reset to Default

To revert to the default Dock settings, click the "Defaults" button.

Tips and Tricks

- Experiment with different settings to find what works best for your workflow and preferences.
- Customize the Dock's appearance and behavior based on your screen size and personal preferences.
- Regularly review and adjust Dock preferences as your needs and usage patterns change.

Clearing the Trash

Step 1: Locating the Trash in the Dock

Look for the Trash icon in the Dock. It resembles a waste bin.

Step 2: Emptying the Trash

Click and hold the Trash icon in the Dock.

A context menu will appear, showing various options.

Step 3: Selecting "Empty Trash"

From the context menu, locate and click the "Empty Trash" option.

A confirmation dialog will appear, asking if you want to delete the Trash items permanently.

Step 4: Confirming the Action

Review the contents of the Trash to ensure you want to proceed.

Click the "Empty Trash" button in the confirmation dialog.

Step 5: Wait for Completion

Your Mac will empty the Trash, permanently deleting all its contents.

The process may take a moment, especially if there are numerous items in the Trash.

Step 6: Notification and Completion

Once the Trash is emptied, you'll receive a notification indicating the action's success.

The Trash icon in the Dock will revert to its default appearance, indicating that it's empty.

Tips and Tricks

- Use caution: The deleted items cannot be recovered once you empty the Trash.
- Securely empty the Trash: For added security, use "Secure Empty Trash" to overwrite deleted files, making them more challenging to recover.
- Review before emptying: Before emptying the Trash, double-check its contents to avoid accidental deletions.

Removing Downloads from the Dock

Step 1: Open the Downloaded File

Locate the downloaded file you want to open.

Double-click on the file to open it with the associated application.

Step 2: Removing the File from the Dock

After you use the file, locate its icon in the Dock.

Click and hold the file icon for a moment.

Step 3: Dragging the File Away

While holding the file icon, drag it away from the Dock.

Move the cursor to a blank area on the desktop or any other location.

Step 4: Releasing the File Icon

Release the mouse button to drop the file icon from the Dock.

The file icon will disappear, indicating that it has been removed.

Step 5: Confirming Removal

Verify that the file has been successfully removed from the Dock if needed.

The Dock should now be free of the file icon you just removed.

Tips and Tricks

- Minimize Dock clutter: Regularly remove file icons from the Dock after using them to keep it clean and organized.
- Organize files: Create dedicated folders on your desktop or in your Documents folder to store files you frequently use instead of keeping them in the Dock.

Dock on Multiple Displays

Step 1: Dock Position Across Displays

Connect additional displays to your MacBook Air 2023.

The Dock can be set to appear on the screen where your cursor is located or on all connected displays simultaneously.

Step 2: Dock Display Options

Click on the Apple menu () in the top-left corner of the screen.

Choose "System Preferences" from the dropdown menu.

Select "Displays."

Click the "Arrangement" tab.

Step 3: Dock Display Preferences

Drag the white rectangle (representing the Dock) to the desired display; this determines where the Dock will appear when using multiple displays.

Step 4: Navigating the Dock Across Displays

Move your cursor to the bottom edge of the display where you positioned the Dock.

The Dock will appear on that display; you can interact with it as usual.

Step 5: Dragging and Launching from the Dock

Drag files, folders, or applications from one display's Dock to another.

Launch applications from the Dock on any connected display.

Step 6: Running Apps and the Dock

Applications that are running will display their icons in the Dock on the active display.

Click on an app icon in the Dock to bring it to the forefront of the active display.

Step 7: Full-Screen Apps and Mission Control

Enter full-screen mode for an app on one display by clicking the green maximize button.

Use Mission Control (three-finger swipe up or "Control + Up Arrow" key) to view and manage full-screen apps across all displays.

Tips and Tricks

- Keep essential apps on the main display's Dock for quick access, even when using multiple displays.
- Customize each display's arrangement to suit your workflow and preferences.
- Experiment with Dock positions and display setups to find what works best.

Keyboard Shortcuts for the Dock

Here's a list of helpful keyboard shortcuts related to the Dock on your MacBook Air 2023:

- **Command + Option + D:** Toggle the visibility of the Dock, showing or hiding it.
- **Command + Tab:** Switch between open applications. Hold down Command and

press Tab repeatedly to cycle through apps, then release to switch to the selected app.

- **Command + Option + Control + D:** Show or hide the definition of the selected word in a floating window.
- **Command + Click:** Right-click (context menu) on an app icon in the Dock to access various options.
- **Option + Click:** Open a new instance of the clicked app in the Dock.
- **Command + H:** Hide the active app.
- **Command + Option + H:** Hide all apps except the currently active one.
- **Command + M:** Minimize the active window to the Dock.
- **Command + Option + M:** Minimize all windows of the currently active app.
- **Command + Shift + T:** Reopen the last closed tab in Safari (or similar action in other web browsers).

- **Command + Shift + 4:** Take a screenshot. You can then drag the crosshair over the Dock to capture a screenshot.
- **Option + Command + D:** Show or hide the Dock's auto-hidden status.
- **Shift + Command + U:** Open the Utilities folder.
- **Shift + Command + H:** Open the Home folder.
- **Shift + Command + D:** Open the Desktop folder.
- **Shift + Command + O:** Open the Documents folder.

Resetting the Dock

Step 1: Open Terminal

Click on the Spotlight icon (magnifying glass) in the top-right corner of the screen.

Type "Terminal" and press "Return" to open the Terminal application.

Step 2: Enter the Command:

In the Terminal window, type the following command:

```
defaults delete com.apple.dock; killall Dock
```

Press "Return" to execute the command.

Step 3: Dock Relaunch

After entering the command, the Dock will automatically relaunch.

The Dock will now be restored to its default settings.

Step 4: Verify Default Settings

Observe the Dock's appearance and behavior.

Icons, positions, and other settings should now match the default configuration.

Tips and Tricks

- Before resetting the Dock, note any customizations you want to recreate after the reset.

- Resetting the Dock will remove any custom app arrangements, hidden icons, and other modifications you've made.

Troubleshooting Dock Issues

1. Apps Not Opening from the Dock

Restart your Mac: Sometimes, a simple restart can resolve app-related issues.

Check for Updates: Ensure your apps are up to date, as outdated software can cause problems.

Reset the Dock: Follow the steps to reset it to its default settings (mentioned in a previous response).

Reinstall Problematic Apps: If a specific app is causing issues, try uninstalling and then reinstalling it.

2. Dock Icons Disappearing or Not Displaying

Restart the Dock: Open Terminal and type `killall Dock` to restart the Dock.

Check Dock Preferences: Go to System Preferences > Dock & Menu Bar and ensure "Automatically hide and show the Dock" is unchecked.

Monitor Resolution: If using multiple displays, ensure your monitor resolutions are correctly set.

3. Auto-Hide Not Working as Expected

Check Dock Preferences: Verify that you have "Automatically hide and show the Dock" enabled in System Preferences > Dock & Menu Bar.

Restart Your MacBook Air: A simple restart can sometimes resolve auto-hide issues.

Reset Dock Preferences: If the problem persists, you can reset the Dock preferences to default settings using Terminal.

4. Stacks Not Organizing Properly

Check Sorting Options: Right-click on a Stack and ensure it's set to the desired sorting method (e.g., Kind, Date Added).

Reset Stacks: Control-click on a Stack and choose "Sort By" > "None" to reset the sorting.

5. Flickering or Glitchy Dock

Update Graphics Drivers: Ensure your graphics drivers are up to date. You can do this through System Preferences > Software Update.

Reset NVRAM/PRAM: Restart your Mac and hold down Option + Command + P + R until you hear the startup sound again.

6. Running Apps Not Displaying Indicator Lights

Check Dock Preferences: In System Preferences,> Dock & Menu Bar, ensure "Show indicators for open applications" is enabled.

Restart the Dock: Use Terminal to restart the Dock using the killall Dock command.

7. Dock Becomes Unresponsive

Force Quit Problematic App: If a specific app is causing the issue, force quit it by pressing Option + Command + Esc.

Restart the Dock: Use Terminal to restart the Dock using the killall Dock command.

Restart Your Mac: If the Dock remains unresponsive, a complete restart of your Mac might be necessary.

8. Inconsistent Dock Appearance Across Displays

Adjust Dock Position: Open System Preferences > Displays > Arrangement and drag the white rectangle (representing the Dock) to the desired display.

9. Customization Changes Not Applying

Restart the Dock: Use Terminal to restart the Dock using the `killall Dock` command.

Log Out and Log In: Sometimes, changes may require a user session refresh.

10. High Dock Resource Usage

Check for Resource-Intensive Apps: Some third-party apps might be causing high resource usage. Monitor your Activity Monitor to identify such apps.

Restart the Dock: Use Terminal to restart the Dock using the `killall Dock` command.

Remember, if you encounter persistent issues that you can't resolve on your own, reaching out to Apple Support or seeking assistance from a technical expert can provide you with more personalized help.

CHAPTER THREE

Connecting External Displays

Step 1: Gather Your Equipment

Before you begin, ensure you have the following items ready:

- Your MacBook Air 2023.
- An external monitor or projector.

- **The appropriate cables:** For most modern monitors or projectors, you'll need a USB-C to HDMI, USB-C to DisplayPort, or USB-C to VGA cable, depending on the available ports.

Step 2: Connect the Cable

Identify the appropriate port on your MacBook Air. It's usually a USB-C port on the left or right side of the device.

Plug one end of the cable into the USB-C port on your MacBook Air.

Connect the other end of the cable to the corresponding port on the external monitor or projector.

Step 3: Configure Display Settings

On your MacBook Air, click the Apple menu () in the top-left corner.

Select "System Preferences."

Choose "Displays."

In the Displays window, navigate to the "Arrangement" tab.

You'll see a representation of your displays. Drag and arrange them according to your preference. You can position the external monitor/projector to the left, right, above, or below your MacBook Air's screen.

Step 4: Adjust Display Preferences

While still in the "Displays" section of System Preferences, click on the "Display" tab.

You can adjust the resolution for each display. Choose "Default for display" or select another that suits your needs.

To optimize the display arrangement, check the "Mirror Displays" box if you want the same content on both screens.

Step 5: Extend Your Display

To extend your display and use the external monitor/projector as a secondary screen, ensure the "Mirror Displays" box is unchecked.

Drag application windows between your MacBook Air's screen and the external monitor/projector to take advantage of the extended workspace.

Tips and Troubleshooting

- If the external display doesn't work, ensure the cable and the monitor/projector function correctly.
- Restart your MacBook Air after connecting the external display for the first time to ensure proper recognition.
- Some apps might not support extended displays by default. Check the app's settings or documentation for compatibility.

Using External Keyboards and Mice

Step 1: Choose Compatible Peripherals

Select an external keyboard and mouse that are compatible with your MacBook Air. Look for models that offer USB-C or Bluetooth connectivity.

Ensure the peripherals have adequate features that suit your preferences, such as ergonomic design, programmable keys, or customizable buttons.

Step 2: Connect the External Keyboard

- For USB-C keyboards:

a. Identify an available USB-C port on your MacBook Air.

b. Plug the USB-C cable from the keyboard into the port.

- For Bluetooth keyboards:

a. On your MacBook Air, click the Apple menu (□) in the top-left corner.

b. Select "System Preferences."

c. Choose "Bluetooth" and ensure it's turned on.

d. Put your keyboard in pairing mode (refer to the keyboard's manual) and wait for it to appear in the Bluetooth devices list.

e. Click on the keyboard's name and follow the prompts to complete pairing.

Step 3: Connect the External Mouse

- For USB-C mice:

a. Locate an available USB-C port on your MacBook Air.

b. Insert the USB-C connector from the mouse into the port.

- For Bluetooth mice:

a. Ensure Bluetooth is enabled on your MacBook Air (System Preferences > Bluetooth).

b. Place your mouse in pairing mode (consult the mouse's manual).

c. When the mouse appears in the Bluetooth devices list, click on its name to pair.

Step 4: Customize Keyboard and Mouse Settings

Access the "System Preferences" from the Apple menu.

Choose "Keyboard" to customize key repeat rate, delay until repeat, and more.

Navigate to "Mouse" or "Trackpad" to adjust tracking speed, scrolling direction, and gesture preferences.

Explore the "Accessibility" section to enable features like Sticky Keys or Mouse Keys for enhanced accessibility.

Step 5: Test and Optimize

Open a text editor to ensure the keyboard is functioning as expected.

Move the external mouse to confirm cursor movement and button responsiveness.

Fine-tune settings in the "Keyboard" and "Mouse" preferences to match your comfort and productivity preferences.

Tips and Troubleshooting:

- Keep your external keyboard and mouse charged or replace batteries regularly for uninterrupted usage.
- If the external keyboard or mouse is not responsive, disconnect and reconnect the cables (if using USB-C) or re-pair (if using Bluetooth).
- Place the Bluetooth peripherals within a reasonable range of your MacBook Air for optimal performance.

Using AirPlay

AirPlay allows you to stream audio and video content from your MacBook Air to compatible devices like Apple TV.

Step 1: Prepare Your Devices

Ensure your MacBook Air 2023 and compatible device (e.g., Apple TV) are connected to the same Wi-Fi network.

Make sure both devices are powered on and ready for communication.

Step 2: Enable AirPlay on MacBook Air

Click the AirPlay icon in the menu bar of your MacBook Air. It looks like a rectangle with an upward-pointing triangle at the bottom.

A menu will appear with a list of available AirPlay devices. Click on the device you want to stream to (e.g., your Apple TV).

Step 3: Stream Audio and Video

- Streaming Audio:

Play the audio content (music, podcast, etc.) on your MacBook Air.

Click the AirPlay icon again and select the desired device from the list.

The audio will start playing on the selected device.

- Streaming Video:

Open the video you want to watch on your MacBook Air.

Click the AirPlay icon and choose the target device from the list.

The video will be mirrored on the larger screen.

Step 4: Adjust Playback and Settings

While streaming, you can control playback (pause, play, skip) from your MacBook Air or an external device.

Adjust the volume using your MacBook Air's volume controls or the controls on the external device.

Step 5: End AirPlay Session

To stop streaming, click the AirPlay icon on your MacBook Air again.

Select "Turn Off AirPlay" or choose your MacBook Air to revert to local playback.

Tips and Troubleshooting:

- Some apps may have built-in AirPlay buttons for quicker access.
- Ensure your MacBook Air and compatible device running the latest software updates for optimal compatibility.
- If you encounter connection issues, check your Wi-Fi network, restart your devices, or temporarily turn off any firewall settings.

Connecting to Wi-Fi Networks

Step 1: Open Network Preferences

Click on the Wi-Fi icon in the menu bar at the top-right corner of your screen (it looks like Wi-Fi signal bars).

From the drop-down menu, select "Open Network Preferences."

Step 2: Choose a Wi-Fi Network

You'll see a list of available Wi-Fi networks in the Network preferences window under "Wi-Fi" on the left.

Click on the name of the Wi-Fi network you want to connect to.

Step 3: Enter Wi-Fi Password

If the selected network is password-protected, a password prompt will appear.

Enter the Wi-Fi password and ensure it's accurate. Passwords are case-sensitive.

Step 4: Connect to the Wi-Fi Network

After entering the correct password, click the "Join" button.

Your MacBook Air will attempt to connect to the selected Wi-Fi network.

Step 5: Verify Connection

Once connected, you'll see a checkmark next to the Wi-Fi network's name in the Network preferences window.

Also, the Wi-Fi icon in the menu bar will display a signal strength indicator.

Step 6: Automatic Connection (Optional)

To automatically connect to this Wi-Fi network whenever it's in range, check the box next to "Remember networks this computer has joined" in the Network preferences.

Step 7: Disconnect from a Wi-Fi Network

If you want to disconnect from the current Wi-Fi network, click the Wi-Fi icon in the menu bar.

Select "Turn Wi-Fi Off."

Tips and Troubleshooting:

- Ensure you have the correct Wi-Fi password. If unsure, ask the network administrator.
- Follow the on-screen instructions if a network requires additional steps (e.g., captive portal login).
- To prioritize Wi-Fi networks, click "Advanced" in Network preferences and adjust the preferred networks list.

Tethering with iPhone

Step 1: Enable Personal Hotspot on iPhone

Unlock your iPhone and go to the "Settings" app.

Scroll down and tap on "Personal Hotspot."

Toggle the switch to turn on Personal Hotspot.

Step 2: Configure Personal Hotspot Settings

After turning on Personal Hotspot, you can customize the Wi-Fi password and other settings.

Create a secure Wi-Fi password that you'll use to connect your MacBook Air.

Step 3: Connect MacBook Air to iPhone's Hotspot

On your MacBook Air, click the Wi-Fi icon in the menu bar (top-right corner).

Look for your iPhone's name in the list of available networks.

Click on your iPhone's name and enter the Wi-Fi password you set in Step 2.

Step 4: Verify Connection

Once connected, you'll see a checkmark next to your iPhone's name in the Wi-Fi menu.

Also, your iPhone's signal strength icon will appear next to the Wi-Fi icon on your MacBook Air.

Step 5: Use the Internet

You can now access the internet with your MacBook Air connected to your iPhone's hotspot.

Launch a web browser, check emails, stream videos, and perform other online tasks as usual.

Step 6: Disable Personal Hotspot (Important)

Return to your iPhone's "Settings" app when you're done using the hotspot.

Tap "Personal Hotspot" and toggle the switch to turn it off.

Tips and Troubleshooting:

- Monitor your iPhone's data usage to avoid exceeding your cellular plan limits.
- If you experience connection issues, restart your iPhone and MacBook Air, then try reconnecting.
- You can also use Bluetooth or USB to connect your MacBook Air to your iPhone's hotspot if Wi-Fi is not preferred.

File Sharing via AirDrop

Step 1: Enable AirDrop on Both Devices

On your MacBook Air, open a Finder window and click "AirDrop" in the sidebar.

A new window will appear. At the bottom of this window, set the visibility to "Everyone" or "Contacts Only," depending on your preferences.

Swipe down from the screen's upper-right corner to access Control Center on your iPhone or other Apple device.

Press and hold the network settings box (Wi-Fi/Bluetooth).

Tap on "AirDrop" and choose "Everyone" or "Contacts Only."

Step 2: Share a File from MacBook Air

Locate the file you want to share on your MacBook Air.

Right-click on the file and select "Share" from the context menu.

In the Share menu, click on the recipient's device under "AirDrop."

Step 3: Accept the AirDrop on the Recipient's Device

A notification on the recipient's Apple device will appear, indicating someone is trying to AirDrop a file.

Tap "Accept" to receive the file.

Step 4: Share a File from iPhone to MacBook Air

Open the app that contains the file you want to share on your iPhone (e.g., Photos, Files).

Select the file you want to share and tap the "Share" button (it looks like an arrow pointing up).

From the sharing options, choose your MacBook Air under the "AirDrop" section.

Step 5: Accept the AirDrop on MacBook Air

On your MacBook Air, a notification will appear, indicating that someone is trying to AirDrop a file.

Click "Accept" to receive the file.

Tips and Troubleshooting:

- Keep both devices within proximity for successful AirDrop transfers.
- If AirDrop doesn't work, ensure that both devices have AirDrop enabled and are connected to the same Wi-Fi network and Bluetooth.
- AirDrop works faster and more reliably when both devices are on the latest software versions.

CHAPTER FOUR

Handoff and Continuity

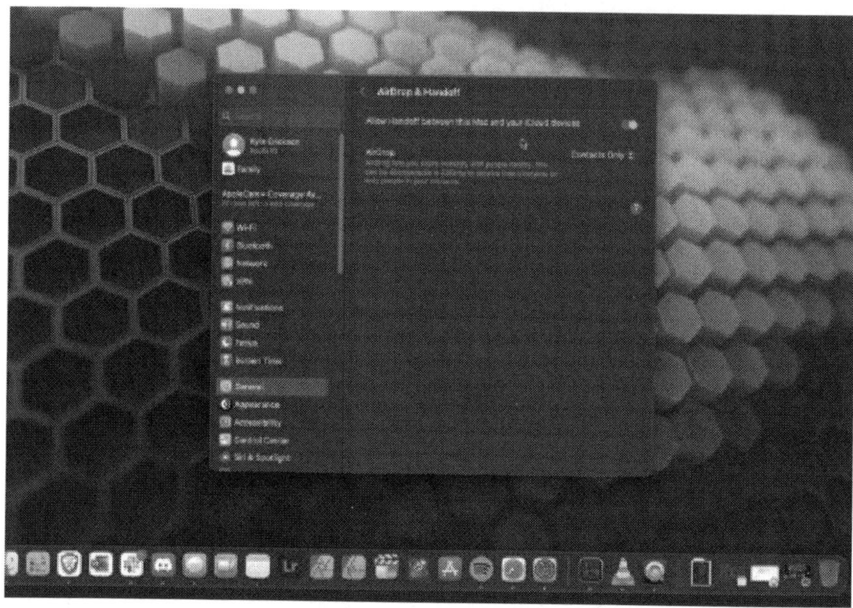

Handoff enables you to start a task on one device and seamlessly continue it on another device, making it perfect for when you're on the move or need a larger screen. Here's how to use Handoff:

Step 1: Ensure Compatibility

Check that all your devices are connected to the same Wi-Fi network and signed in with the same Apple ID.

Verify that Handoff is enabled on each device. On your MacBook Air, go to "System Preferences" > "General" and ensure "Allow Handoff between this Mac and your iCloud devices" is checked. On other devices, go to "Settings" > "General" > "AirPlay & Handoff" and turn on Handoff.

Step 2: Start a Task

Begin a task on one of your devices, such as composing an email or browsing a webpage.

Step 3: Continue on Another Device

Pick up your other Apple device that is nearby and unlocked.

Look for the app's icon on the device's lock screen or in the app switcher (double-click the home button or swipe up from the bottom of the screen).

Continuity

Continuity expands the Handoff concept by allowing your MacBook Air and other Apple devices to work seamlessly. Here's how to use Continuity:

Step 1: Make and Receive Calls

Ensure your MacBook Air and iPhone are on the same Wi-Fi network and signed in with the same Apple ID.

On your MacBook Air, go to "FaceTime" > "Preferences" and check "Calls from iPhone."

Step 2: Make and Receive Texts

On your MacBook Air, go to "Messages" > "Preferences" and check "Text Message Forwarding." Follow the on-screen instructions to complete the setup.

Step 3: Universal Clipboard

With Continuity, you can copy text, images, or files on one device and paste them on another.

Copy content on your MacBook Air, which will be available to paste on your other Apple devices and vice versa.

Universal Clipboard

Step 1: Check Compatibility and Sign In

Ensure your MacBook Air and iOS devices (iPhone, iPad) use the same Apple ID.

Ensure your device is running iOS 10 or later on your iOS devices.

Step 2: Enable Bluetooth and Wi-Fi

On your MacBook Air, click the Wi-Fi icon in the menu bar (top-right corner) and ensure Wi-Fi is turned on.

On your iOS device, go to "Settings" > "Bluetooth" and ensure Bluetooth is enabled.

Step 3: Enable Handoff and Universal Clipboard

On your MacBook Air, go to "System Preferences" > "General."

Ensure "Allow Handoff between this Mac and your iCloud devices" is checked.

On your iOS device, go to "Settings" > "General" > "AirPlay & Handoff" and turn on Handoff.

Step 4: Copy and Paste with Universal Clipboard

Copy any text, image, or file using the usual copy command (Command+C) on your MacBook Air.

On your iOS device, open any app where you want to paste the copied content.

Double-tap or long-press the text field where you want to paste, then tap "Paste."

Step 5: Copy and Paste from iOS to MacBook Air

Copy any content on your iOS device (text, image, or file).

On your MacBook Air 2023, open the destination app or document.

Use the paste command (Command+V) to paste the content.

Syncing with iCloud

Step 1: Sign In to iCloud

On your MacBook Air 2023, click the Apple menu () in the top-left corner.

Select "System Preferences" and then click "Apple ID."

If you're not signed in, click "Sign In" and enter your Apple ID and password. If you don't have an Apple ID, you can create one.

Step 2: Choose What to Sync

In the Apple ID preferences, click "iCloud" in the left sidebar.

Check the boxes next to "Photos," "Contacts," and "Calendars" to enable syncing for these items.

Step 3: Sync Photos

In the iCloud preferences, click the "Options" button next to "Photos."

Select "iCloud Photos" to enable syncing; this will keep your photos and videos up-to-date across all devices.

You can optimize storage on your MacBook Air to save space by storing full-resolution photos and videos in iCloud.

Step 4: Sync Contacts

In the iCloud preferences, ensure that "Contacts" is selected.

Any changes you make to your contacts on any device will automatically sync with all your other devices.

Step 5: Sync Calendars

In the iCloud preferences, make sure "Calendars" is selected.

Any events or appointments you add or modify in your calendars will be synced across your devices.

Step 6: Check Syncing Status

To check if your data is syncing, click the Apple menu (□) in the top-left corner of your MacBook Air.

Select "System Preferences" > "Apple ID" > "iCloud."

You'll see a list of items that are being synced with iCloud. Ensure that "Photos," "Contacts," and "Calendars" have checkmarks next to them.

Using Sidecar

Step 1: Compatibility Check

Make sure your MacBook Air and iPad meet the system requirements for Sidecar:

- MacBook Air 2023

- iPad: Sixth-generation iPad or later, iPad Air (third generation), iPad mini (fifth generation), or any iPad Pro

Step 2: Set Up Sidecar

Ensure your MacBook Air and iPad are signed in to the same Apple ID and connected to the same Wi-Fi network and Bluetooth.

On your MacBook Air, click the Apple menu (□) in the top-left corner, then choose "System Preferences."

Select "Displays."

Go to the "Arrangement" tab.

A checkbox labeled "Show displays in the menu bar." Check this box to make the Displays menu accessible from the menu bar.

Step 3: Activate Sidecar

On your MacBook Air, click the Displays icon in the menu bar (it looks like a rectangle with a triangle at the bottom).

From the dropdown menu, select your iPad under the "Connect to" section.

Step 4: Choose Sidecar Mode

Once connected, you can choose from two modes:

"Mirror Display": Your iPad will mirror the content on your MacBook Air's screen.

"Use As Separate Display": Your iPad becomes an extended display, giving you a second screen for multitasking.

Step 5: Touch and Pencil Interactions (Optional)

If using an Apple Pencil, you can interact with the content on your iPad's screen, allowing for precise input and drawing capabilities.

Use your fingers on the iPad's screen as on any touch device to enable touch input.

Managing External Storage Devices

Step 1: Connecting External Storage Devices

Locate an available USB-C port on your MacBook Air.

Plug your USB drive, SSD, or external hard drive into the port. Some devices may require an adapter for compatibility.

Step 2: Recognizing and Mounting the Device

Once connected, your MacBook Air should detect the external storage device.

A device icon will appear on your desktop, or you can access it through Finder in the sidebar under "Devices."

Step 3: Transferring Files

Open a Finder window and navigate to the location of the files you want to transfer.

Drag and drop the files onto the external storage device icon.

Step 4: Ejecting the External Storage Device

To safely remove the external storage device, click its icon on the desktop or Finder.

Click the eject button (an upward-pointing arrow) next to the device's name.

Step 5: Managing External Storage Devices

To check the available space on the external storage device, right-click its icon and select "Get Info."

Use the "Format" option (found by right-clicking the device icon) to change the file system format if needed. Be cautious, as formatting erases all data.

Step 6: Managing Files and Folders

Organize your files on the external storage device as you would on your MacBook Air's internal drive.

Create new folders, move files, and maintain a structured organization.

Step 7: Safely Eject the External Storage Device

Before physically unplugging the device, ensure it's properly ejected by clicking the eject button next to its name in Finder.

Tips and Troubleshooting:

- Use USB-C hubs or adapters if your external storage device uses a different connector type.
- Keep your external storage devices safe and clean to prevent damage; always back up important data from your external storage devices to avoid loss.

Printing from MacBook Air

Step 1: Determine Printer Compatibility

Check if your printer is compatible with macOS by visiting the manufacturer's website or referring to the printer's manual.

Step 2: Connect the Printer

- For Wired Printers:

Connect your printer to your MacBook Air using a USB cable.

Please turn on the printer and ensure it's properly connected.

- For Wireless Printers:

Connect your printer to your Wi-Fi network using the printer's setup menu or instructions provided by the manufacturer.

Make sure your MacBook Air is connected to the same Wi-Fi network.

Step 3: Add Printer on MacBook Air

Click the Apple menu (□) in the top-left corner of your screen.

Select "System Preferences" > "Printers & Scanners."

Click the "+" button to add a new printer.

Your printer should appear in the list of available devices. Select it and click "Add."

Step 4: Set Printer Preferences

In the Printers & Scanners preferences, select your printer from the list on the left.

Click the "Options & Supplies" or "Open Print Queue" button to access printer settings.

Configure paper size, quality, and other printing preferences as needed.

Step 5: Test Printing

Open a document or image you want to print.

Choose "File" > "Print" or use the Command+P shortcut.

Select your printer from the dropdown menu.

Adjust any print settings if necessary.

Click "Print" to send the job to the printer.

Step 6: Troubleshooting and Maintenance

If your printer doesn't appear in the list, ensure it's properly connected and turned on.

Check for software updates for your printer on the manufacturer's website.

Clear paper jams, replace ink cartridges, and perform routine maintenance to ensure optimal print quality.

Tips:

- Some printers may require specific drivers or software to work with macOS. Check the manufacturer's website for compatibility and driver downloads.
- Consider setting your printer as the default printer for easier access in the future.

Using External CD/DVD Drives

Step 1: Choose a Compatible External CD/DVD Drive

Select an external CD/DVD drive compatible with both macOS and your MacBook Air model.

Look for drives with USB connectivity, as USB is a standard interface for external purposes.

Step 2: Connect the External CD/DVD Drive

Plug the USB cable from the external CD/DVD drive into an available USB port on your MacBook Air.

Ensure the drive is powered on and any necessary power cables are connected.

Step 3: Reading Discs

Insert the disc (CD/DVD) you want to read into the external drive.

The disc should mount on your desktop or appear in Finder.

Step 4: Accessing Disc Contents

Open Finder and navigate to the mounted disc icon on your desktop or the sidebar.

Browse the contents of the disc and open files or folders as needed.

Step 5: Burning Discs

Create a new folder on your desktop or Finder to organize the files you want to burn onto a disc.

Drag and drop the files you wish to burn into the new folder.

Step 6: Prepare for Burning

Right-click (or Control-click) the folder containing the files and select "Burn [folder name] to Disc."

A burning window will appear, prompting you to configure disc settings.

Step 7: Configure Burning Options

Enter a name for the disc.

Select the burning speed (a lower rate is often better for compatibility).

Choose the format if prompted (usually "Mastered" for read-only discs and "Live File System" for rewritable discs).

Step 8: Initiate Burning

Click the "Burn" button to start the burning process.

The progress and completion status will be displayed.

Step 9: Eject the Disc

Once burning is complete or you're finished reading the disc, eject it by clicking the eject button next to the disc's name in Finder or on the desktop.

Tips and Troubleshooting:

- Ensure the external CD/DVD drive is powered on and connected adequately before attempting to read or burn discs.
- Some discs may not be compatible with specific drives. Check the drive's compatibility before inserting a disc.
- For optimal burning quality, use high-quality blank discs and burn at a lower speed if necessary.

Using SD Cards

Step 1: Inserting and Ejecting the SD Card

Locate the SD card slot on your MacBook Air. It is usually situated on the right-hand side.

Gently push the SD card into the slot, ensuring it is appropriately aligned. Please do not force it; the card should slide in smoothly.

Locate the eject button next to the card slot to eject the SD card. Press the button, and the card will pop out slightly. You can then pull it out with your fingers.

Step 2: Transferring Data to and from the SD Card

Once the SD card is inserted, your MacBook Air will automatically detect it. A new icon representing the SD card will appear on your desktop.

Double-click the SD card icon to open its contents. You'll see folders and files, just like you would with any other storage device.

To transfer files from your MacBook Air to the SD card, drag and drop them from your computer's folders onto the SD card's window. Wait for the transfer to complete.

To move files from the SD card to your MacBook Air, select the desired files on the SD card, drag them to the location on your computer where you want them, and release the mouse button.

Step 3: Safely Ejecting the SD Card

Before physically removing the SD card, make sure you've closed any files or applications that were using the card.

Click the SD card icon on your desktop to select it.

Go to the "File" menu at the top of your screen and choose "Eject [SD Card Name]." Alternatively, right-click the SD card icon and select "Eject."

Once the card is safely ejected, gently press the eject button near the card slot to pop it out slightly, then remove it from the place.

Tips:

- Always handle SD cards with care and avoid touching the metal connectors.
- Ejecting the SD card before physically removing it is recommended to prevent data loss or corruption.
- If you encounter any issues, restart your MacBook Air and try the process again.

Connecting to Ethernet

Step 1: Gather the Necessary Equipment

MacBook Air 2023.

USB-C Ethernet adapter, compatible with MacBook Air.

Ethernet cable (RJ45) with the appropriate length for your setup.

Step 2: Setting Up the Ethernet Adapter

Plug the USB-C end of the Ethernet adapter into any available USB-C port on your MacBook Air.

Connect the Ethernet cable (RJ45) to the Ethernet port of the adapter.

Ensure that the Ethernet adapter is securely connected to your MacBook Air and the Ethernet cable is plugged into a functioning Ethernet port on your network.

Step 3: Connecting to a Wired Network

On your MacBook Air, click on the Apple menu () in the top-left corner of your screen.

Select "System Preferences" from the dropdown menu.

In the System Preferences window, click on "Network."

You should see a list of available network connections in the Network preferences on the left. Click the "+" button at the bottom left to add a new link.

A pop-up window will appear. From the "Interface" dropdown menu, select "USB Ethernet" or a similar option based on your adapter.

In the "Name" field, you can give your connection a meaningful name, like "Wired Connection."

Click the "Create" button to add the new network connection.

You should now see your newly added "Wired Connection" or similar option on the left in the Network preferences. Select it.

In the right-hand pane, ensure "Configure IPv4" is set to "Using DHCP" for automatic network configuration.

Your MacBook Air will automatically attempt to connect to the wired network using the Ethernet adapter. Once connected, you'll see a green dot next to the connection name.

Step 4: Testing the Connection

Open a web browser or any online application to ensure an active internet connection.

Visit a website to confirm that you can browse the internet without issues.

Tips:

- If you're experiencing connectivity problems, try restarting your MacBook Air and checking cable connections.

- To disconnect from the wired network, click the network connection in the Network preferences and click the "Disconnect" button.

Virtualization and Boot Camp

Virtualization allows you to run an operating system (OS) within another OS, effectively creating a virtual environment. One of the most popular virtualization software options for macOS is Parallels Desktop. Here's what you need to know:

- Benefits:

Convenience: Virtualization lets you switch between macOS and the guest OS (e.g., Windows) seamlessly without rebooting your MacBook Air.

Parallel Operation: You can run both macOS and the guest OS simultaneously, using applications from both environments simultaneously.

- Considerations:

Resource Allocation: Running a virtual machine can consume significant system resources, potentially impacting overall performance.

Licensing: You'll need a valid license for the guest OS you're virtualizing.

Compatibility: Not all applications or features may work seamlessly within a virtual environment.

- Steps:

Choose Virtualization Software: Download and install virtualization software like Parallels Desktop.

Install Guest OS: Follow the software's instructions to create a virtual machine and install the guest OS (e.g., Windows).

Integration: Install any necessary drivers or tools the virtualization software provides to enhance integration between macOS and the guest OS.

- **Boot Camp**

Boot Camp is a built-in utility provided by Apple that allows you to install and run a separate operating system on a separate partition of your MacBook Air's storage. Here's what you should know:

- Benefits:

Native Performance: Boot Camp provides access to the entire hardware resources of your MacBook Air, resulting in optimal performance for the guest OS.

Gaming and High-Performance Applications: If you're interested in gaming or resource-intensive applications, Boot Camp may offer a better experience.

- Considerations:

Reboot Required: You must reboot your MacBook Air to switch between macOS and the guest OS.

Partitioning: Creating a separate partition for the guest OS will reduce your available storage for macOS.

Driver Compatibility: Ensure you have the necessary drivers for your MacBook Air's hardware components to work within the guest OS.

- Steps:

Check Compatibility: Ensure your MacBook Air model is compatible with Boot Camp.

Prepare Bootable Media: Create a bootable USB drive or disc containing the installation files for the guest OS (e.g., Windows).

Run Boot Camp Assistant: Open Boot Camp Assistant (found in the Applications > Utilities folder) and follow the on-screen instructions to partition your drive and install the guest OS.

Install Drivers: After installing the guest OS, install the necessary drivers' Boot Camp to ensure proper hardware functionality.

External Device Security

Connecting external devices to your MacBook Air can significantly enhance its functionality. Still, it's essential to safeguard your data and maintain the security of your system.

1. Keep Your Software Updated

Regularly update your MacBook Air's operating system (macOS) and all installed software, including security. Updates often include patches for known vulnerabilities that attackers might exploit.

2. Use Reliable External Devices

Purchase external devices from reputable manufacturers and sources. Cheap or counterfeit devices might come with hidden security risks.

3. Enable Firewalls

Activate the built-in firewall on your MacBook Air to monitor and block suspicious network traffic. Go to

System Preferences > Security & Privacy > Firewall to enable it.

4. Use Strong Passwords

Ensure you have a strong password for your MacBook Air user account and any important accounts linked to external devices. A strong password includes upper and lower-case letters, numbers, and special characters.

5. Encrypt Your Data

Enable FileVault, a built-in macOS feature that encrypts your entire disk; this ensures that your data remains protected even if an external device is compromised. Go to System Preferences > Security & Privacy > FileVault to enable it.

6. Disable AutoRun/AutoPlay

Turn off auto-run/auto-play for external devices; this prevents potential malware from automatically executing when you connect a device.

7. Scan for Malware

Use reputable antivirus and anti-malware software to scan external devices for potential threats before accessing their content.

8. Avoid Public Computers

If you need to connect external devices to other computers, avoid public computers or untrusted systems that might be compromised.

9. Safely Eject Devices

Always eject external devices properly before physically disconnecting them. Abruptly removing a device can corrupt data or damage the device itself.

10. Backup Your Data

Regularly back up your MacBook Air's data to an external or cloud storage. You'll have a copy of your essential files in case of a security breach or device failure.

11. Disable Unneeded Services

Turn off any unnecessary services or features on your MacBook Air that could provide an entry point for attackers.

12. Educate Yourself

Stay informed about the latest security practices and potential threats. Educate yourself and your users about phishing, social engineering, and other standard attack methods.

CHAPTER FIVE

Using MIDI Controllers

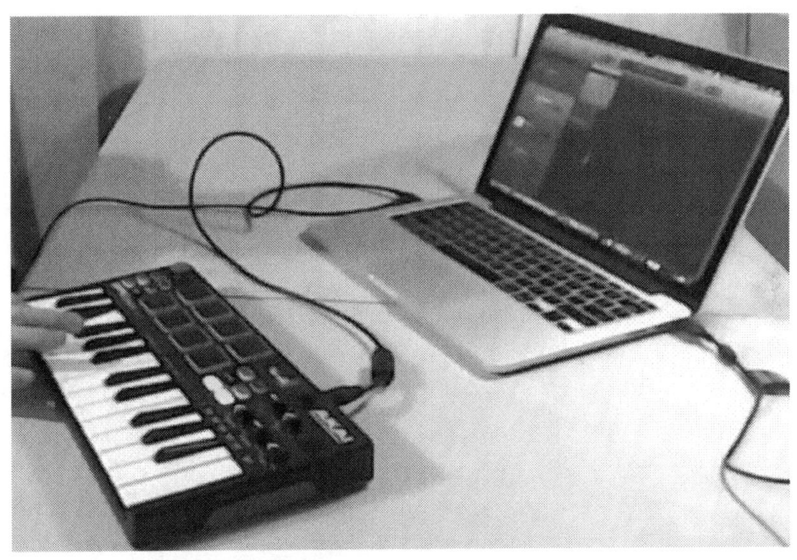

Step 1: Understand MIDI and MIDI Controllers

MIDI (Musical Instrument Digital Interface) is a protocol that allows electronic musical instruments and devices to communicate. MIDI controllers, such as keyboards, pads, and knobs, transmit MIDI data to control software instruments and parameters.

Choose a MIDI controller that suits your needs and budget. Consider factors like the number of keys, pads, knobs, and compatibility with your music software.

Step 2: Gather the Required Hardware and Software

Ensure your MacBook Air is powered off and disconnected from power sources or peripherals.

Identify the type of MIDI connection your controller uses: USB, MIDI over Bluetooth, or traditional MIDI ports (requires a MIDI-to-USB adapter).

Install any required drivers or software provided by the MIDI controller manufacturer.

Step 3: Connect the MIDI Controller

- For USB MIDI controllers:

Plug the USB cable from the MIDI controller into an available USB port on your MacBook Air.

MacOS should automatically recognize your MIDI controller.

- For MIDI over Bluetooth controllers:

Enable Bluetooth on your MacBook Air and put your MIDI controller into pairing mode.

Pair the MIDI controller with your MacBook Air using the Bluetooth menu in the menu bar.

- For traditional MIDI controllers (using a MIDI-to-USB adapter):

Connect the MIDI-out cable from the controller to the MIDI-in port of the adapter.

Connect the MIDI-in cable from the controller to the MIDI-out port of the adapter.

Plug the USB end of the adapter into an available USB port on your MacBook Air.

Step 4: Configure MIDI Settings in Music Software

Open your preferred music production software (Logic Pro, Ableton Live, GarageBand, etc.).

Access the MIDI settings or preferences within the software.

Locate the MIDI input section and select your connected MIDI controller as the input device.

As desired, map the MIDI controller's buttons, keys, and knobs to software functions or instruments.

Step 5: Test and Create Music

Load a virtual instrument or software synthesizer into your music software.

Play the keys or pads on your MIDI controller to trigger sounds from the software instrument.

Experiment with different instrument presets and effects using the MIDI controller's knobs and sliders.

Step 6: Perform Live with Your MIDI Controller

Set up your MacBook Air and MIDI controller on a stable surface for live performances.

Prepare your music software with the desired setlist and instrument configurations.

Practice performing with the MIDI controller to ensure smooth transitions and expressive control.

External Webcams

Suppose you want to elevate your video calls, online meetings, or recordings to a professional level. In that case, an external webcam can significantly affect video quality.

Step 1: Choose the Right External Webcam

Research and select an external webcam that suits your needs and budget. Look for high-resolution (1080p or higher) features, autofocus, and low-light performance.

Ensure the webcam is compatible with macOS and your MacBook Air model.

Step 2: Prepare Your MacBook Air and Webcam

Shut down your MacBook Air and disconnect any power sources or peripherals.

Connect the USB cable from the external webcam to an available USB port on your MacBook Air.

Step 3: Position and Set Up the External Webcam

Place the external webcam on a stable surface, ideally at eye level or slightly above, for a more flattering and natural angle.

Adjust the webcam's focus and framing to ensure you're visible in the frame.

If necessary, use the webcam's built-in settings or software (if provided) to fine-tune image settings like brightness, contrast, and color balance.

Step 4: Configure Video Settings in Video Call or Recording Software

Open your preferred video conferencing or recording software (e.g., Zoom, Microsoft Teams, OBS Studio, etc.).

Access the video settings or preferences within the software.

Choose the external webcam as your preferred video input source.

Adjust video settings like resolution and frame rate according to your webcam's capabilities.

Step 5: Test and Optimize Video Quality

Initiate a video call with a friend or colleague, or start a test recording.

Pay attention to the video quality, focusing on clarity, color accuracy, and low-light performance.

If necessary, adjust the webcam settings and lighting conditions for optimal results.

Step 6: Additional Tips for Improved Video Quality

Ensure adequate lighting in your environment. Natural light or soft, diffused artificial lighting can enhance your appearance on camera.

Consider using an external microphone for improved audio quality, especially if your MacBook Air's built-in microphone doesn't meet your needs.

Use a clutter-free and visually appealing background to maintain a professional appearance during video calls and recordings.

Using Your iPhone as a WebCam

Before delving into the setup process, ensure your MacBook Air 2023 has macOS Ventura. Additionally, your iPhone should be an eight or XR model or a more recent version, all operating on iOS 16.

Both devices must be logged into the same Apple ID account, with Wi-Fi and Bluetooth functionalities activated. Moreover, if you wish to capitalize on the Center Stage and Desk View attributes, an iPhone 11 or later is essential.

At the same time, the Studio Light function necessitates an iPhone 12 or newer. Lastly, acquiring a camera mount capable of securely positioning your iPhone atop your Mac's display is recommended.

Step 1: Activating the Continuity Camera on your iPhone

Commence by launching the Settings app on your iPhone. Navigate to General > AirPlay & Handoff, then toggle the switch for the Continuity Camera Webcam option. Once this is done, exit the Settings menu. Securely position your iPhone on MacBook's display using a holder, mount, tripod, or any other method of your preference, ensuring the Bluetooth connection between the devices remains active.

Step 2: Launch a video application on your MacBook Air

Invoke the video application of your choice on your MacBook Air –FaceTime, Zoom, or another option like QuickTime, which we'll use for this demonstration. Upon launching the app, locate the camera selection setting, typically found adjacent to the record button. Within QuickTime, it appears as a dropdown menu. Your iPhone's name should be listed among the available cameras. Select your iPhone, and voila! Your MacBook now employs the iPhone as its webcam. You may also have the option to designate the iPhone's microphone as the audio input device, with the exact location varying depending on the application.

Step 3: Enabling Desk View

Desk View utilizes the iPhone's Ultra Wide camera (requires iPhone 11 or newer) to capture a view of your workspace. It's important to note that Desk View maintains a fixed angle, which doesn't encompass the MacBook keyboard if the iPhone is affixed to the laptop's display. Instead, it captures the area roughly a foot in front of the computer.

As of now, Apple has not confirmed whether the angle will be adjustable in future updates. To activate Desk View, ensure Continuity Camera is operational. Access the Control Center in the menu bar and select the Video Effects button, which is only visible when the camera is active. From the ensuing Video Effects menu, opt for Desk View. This same menu is also where you can deactivate Desk View.

Upon selecting Desk View, an accompanying app will launch. To simultaneously view your video application and Desk View, you can experiment with window tiling (Window > Tile Window to Left/Right Side of Screen). This tiling feature might not be compatible with specific applications like FaceTime.

Step 4: Engaging Center Stage

Center Stage, an engaging feature that ensures you remain centered in the frame (requires iPhone 11 or newer), is easily accessible. With Continuity Camera engaged, access the Control Center from the menu bar and click the Video Effects button; this will unveil a menu of video effects, within which you can activate Center Stage.

Step 5: Utilizing Portrait Mode

Portrait mode, which artfully blurs the background, is another attractive option. In the Control Center in the menu bar, click the Video Effects button, and choose Portrait from the ensuing menu. This action will induce a pleasing background blur.

Step 6: Harnessing Studio Light

For those seeking enhanced illumination, Studio Light utilizes the iPhone's flash to brighten your image (requires iPhone 12 or newer). Like the previous steps, activate Continuity Camera and access the Control Center from the menu bar. Click on the Video Effects button and select Studio Light.

Step 7: Disengaging your iPhone as the Mac's webcam

Should you wish to revert to the default webcam or conclude your usage, exit the video application on your Mac. Your iPhone may exhibit a screen similar to the one depicted above; a single tap on "Disconnect" will effectively terminate the connection.

By adhering to these steps and embracing the innovative Continuity Camera feature, you can seamlessly integrate your iPhone with your MacBook Air, enriching your video communication experience.

Using VPNs and Network Drives

Step 1: Set Up a VPN Connection

Research a reputable VPN service that meets your security and privacy needs.

Download and install the VPN client software the chosen service provides on your MacBook Air.

Step 2: Configure and Connect to the VPN

Launch the VPN client software.

Log in to your VPN account using the credentials provided by the service.

Choose a VPN server location based on your preferences (e.g., closer to your physical location for better performance).

Click the "Connect" button to establish a secure VPN connection.

Step 3: Access Network Drives Remotely

Determine if your organization or network offers a remote access solution for network drives (e.g., VPN-based access or a cloud-based solution).

If using a VPN-based approach, ensure your VPN connection is active before proceeding.

Step 4: Map Network Drives

Open "Finder" on your MacBook Air.

Go to the "Go" menu and select "Connect to Server."

In the "Server Address" field, enter the network drive's address using the appropriate format (e.g., smb://servername/sharename for Windows-based networks or afp://servername/sharename for Apple File Protocol).

Click the "Connect" button.

Step 5: Authenticate and Access Network Drives

You'll be prompted to enter your credentials (username and password) for accessing the network drive.

Optionally, select the "Remember this password in my keychain" checkbox to avoid repeated authentication.

Click the "Connect" button to access the network drive.

Step 6: Secure File Sharing and Remote Work

With the VPN connection established and network drives accessible, you can securely share and access files as if you were on-site.

Use your favorite file management software (e.g., Finder, Windows File Explorer) to copy, move, and edit files on the network drive.

Remember to disconnect from the VPN when your remote work is complete to ensure your internet traffic returns to standard routing.

Tips:

- Regularly update your VPN client and network drive access methods for security patches.
- Use strong, unique passwords for both your VPN and network drive accounts.
- Be cautious when accessing sensitive files remotely, and avoid public Wi-Fi networks for added security.

Remote Desktop and Screen Sharing

Step 1: Enable Screen Sharing on Your MacBook Air 2023

Open "System Preferences" from the Apple menu.

Click on "Sharing."

Check the "Screen Sharing" checkbox to enable this feature.

If desired, click the "Computer Settings" button to configure access options and security settings.

Step 2: Access Remote Desktop or Screen Sharing

Open "Finder" on your MacBook Air.

In the menu bar, select "Go" and then "Connect to Server."

Enter the network address of the computer you want to access using one of the following formats:

For Remote Desktop (Microsoft Windows): vnc://computername or vnc://IPaddress

For Screen Sharing (Mac computers): vnc://computername.local or vnc://IPaddress

Click the "Connect" button.

Step 3: Authenticate and Connect

You'll be prompted to enter your credentials (username and password) for accessing the remote computer.

Optionally, select the "Remember this password in my keychain" checkbox for future convenience.

Click the "Connect" button to establish the remote connection.

Step 4: Control the Remote Computer

Once connected, you'll see the remote computer's screen on your MacBook Air.

Use your mouse and keyboard to control the remote computer as if you were physically present.

You can transfer files between your local and remote computer, copy and paste text, and perform various tasks seamlessly.

Step 5: Allow Remote Access to Your MacBook Air

If you want to allow someone else to access your MacBook Air remotely:

Open "System Preferences" and click on "Sharing."

Check the "Screen Sharing" checkbox to enable remote access.

Share your computer's address or IP with the person accessing your MacBook Air.

Step 6: Disconnect and Secure Remote Access

To end the remote session, close the Screen Sharing window or click the close button on the top of the screen.

If you allow remote access to your MacBook Air, turn off Screen Sharing when you no longer need it for security reasons.

Tips:

- Ensure that both computers have stable internet connections for smoother remote access.
- Consider using a secure Virtual Private Network (VPN) for an added layer of protection during remote connections.
- If you encounter connectivity issues, check firewall settings and ensure both computers have Screen Sharing or Remote Desktop enabled.

Apple Pencil and iPad Integration

Step 1: Prepare Your Devices

Ensure your MacBook Air, Apple Pencil, and iPad are charged and powered on.

Sign in to the same iCloud account on all devices for seamless synchronization.

Step 2: Pair Apple Pencil with Your iPad

Remove the cap from your Apple Pencil and plug it into your iPad's Lightning or USB-C port.

Follow the on-screen instructions to pair and connect your Apple Pencil to your iPad.

Step 3: Set Up Handoff Between MacBook Air and iPad

On your MacBook Air, open "System Preferences."

Click on "General" and ensure "Allow Handoff between this Mac and your iCloud devices" is checked.

On your iPad, go to "Settings" > "General" > "Handoff" and ensure it's enabled.

Step 4: Note-Taking and Document Collaboration

Open a note-taking app like Apple Notes on your iPad.

Use your Apple Pencil to jot down handwritten notes, create sketches, and highlight text.

Switch to your MacBook Air as you work, and an icon for your note will appear in the Dock. Click it to continue your work on the MacBook Air seamlessly.

Collaborate by sharing notes with others through iCloud; they can access and edit the same messages on their devices.

Step 5: Digital Drawing and Illustration

Launch a drawing app like Procreate on your iPad.

Use your Apple Pencil to create stunning digital artwork with precise strokes and varying levels of pressure sensitivity.

Leverage iPad's large touch screen and Apple Pencil's responsive design to refine your artistic vision.

Use Handoff to effortlessly transfer your work to your MacBook Air for further refinement or sharing.

Step 6: Seamless Creative Workflow

Create a presentation or design on your MacBook Air using Keynote or Adobe Creative Cloud software.

Import your creation to your iPad using AirDrop or iCloud Drive.

Annotate, highlight or add freehand sketches using your Apple Pencil on your iPad.

Utilize Handoff to continue editing the project on your MacBook Air, ensuring a consistent and efficient creative workflow.

Using Handwriting Recognition

Handwriting recognition allows you to seamlessly bridge the gap between your MacBook Air and compatible devices like iPads, transforming handwritten notes into digital ones.

Step 1: Prepare Your Devices

Ensure your MacBook Air and iPad are charged and powered on.

Sign in to the same iCloud account on both devices for seamless synchronization.

Step 2: Enable Handwriting Recognition on iPad

On your iPad, open "Settings."

Scroll down and tap on "Apple Pencil & Keyboard."

Enable "Scribble" to activate handwriting recognition on your iPad.

Step 3: Write and Convert Handwritten Notes

Use your Apple Pencil to write handwritten notes in apps like Notes or Pages on your iPad.

Scribble recognizes your handwriting and converts it into editable text in real-time.

Step 4: Access Handwritten Notes on MacBook Air

On your MacBook Air, ensure you're signed in to the same iCloud account as your iPad.

Open the "Notes" app to access your synchronized handwritten notes.

Step 5: Edit and Refine Handwritten Text

Once your handwritten notes are on your MacBook Air, you can edit, format, and refine the converted text using your keyboard.

Correct any recognition errors and enhance the readability of your notes.

Step 6: Synchronize Changes

Any changes to the converted text on your MacBook Air will be synchronized to your iPad via iCloud.

Similarly, changes made on your iPad will also be reflected on your MacBook Air.

Tips:

- Practice neat and legible handwriting to enhance the accuracy of handwriting recognition.
- Use your Apple Pencil to add annotations or sketches alongside the converted text for visual context.
- Explore third-party note-taking apps that offer advanced handwriting recognition features.

CHAPTER SIX

Smart Home Integration

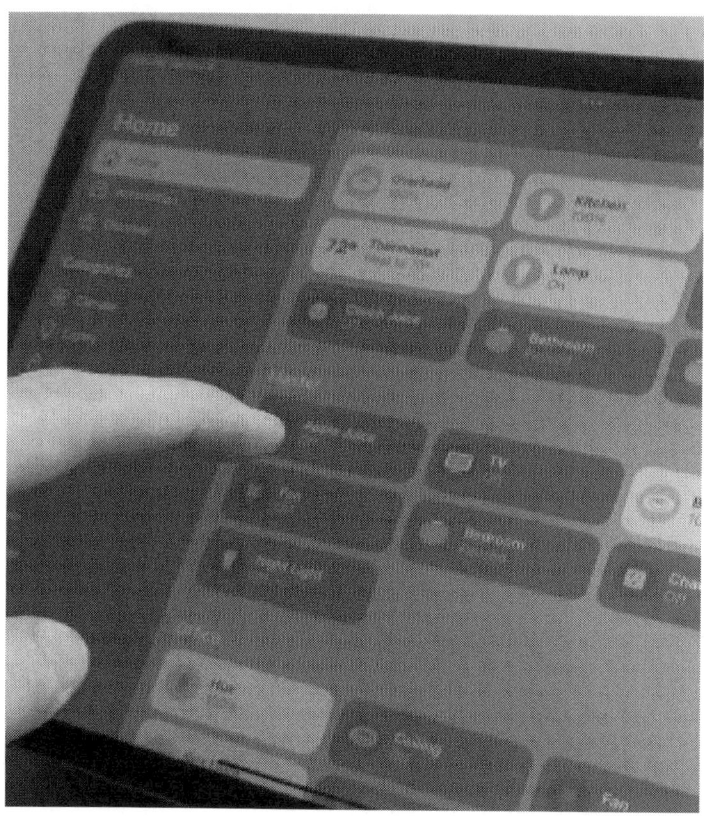

Step 1: Set Up Your Smart Home Ecosystem

Before you can control your smart devices, ensure that your smart home ecosystem is adequately set up:

- Select Compatible Devices: Choose home devices compatible with your MacBook Air. Look for devices that support Apple HomeKit or have dedicated macOS apps.
- Connect to Wi-Fi: Make sure all your smart devices are connected to the same Wi-Fi network as your MacBook Air. A stable network connection is crucial for seamless communication.
- Install Required Apps: Visit the Mac App Store to download and install apps essential for controlling your specific devices. Standard apps include "Home" for Apple HomeKit-compatible devices or dedicated apps provided by device manufacturers.

Step 2: Connect and Configure Your Devices

Now that your smart home ecosystem is set up, it's time to connect and configure your devices:

- Open the App: Launch the app you installed for controlling your smart devices.

- Add Devices: Look for an option to add or discover new devices within the app. Follow the on-screen instructions to pair with your MacBook Air; this usually involves scanning a QR code or using device-specific pairing methods.
- Arrange Devices: Organize your devices within the app by assigning them to specific rooms or zones; this helps you manage and control multiple devices more efficiently.

Step 3: Control Your Smart Home Devices

With your devices connected and configured, you can now start controlling them:

- Access Control Center: On your MacBook Air, click the Control Center icon in the menu bar (located at the top-right corner); this provides quick access to essential home controls.
- Interact with Devices: You can directly interact with your smart devices from the Control Center. For example, adjust the

brightness of the lights, control the thermostat, or lock/unlock high-tech locks.

- Use Voice Commands (Optional): If you have a compatible virtual assistant like Siri, you can control your smart devices using voice commands. Activate Siri by clicking the icon in the menu bar or using a keyboard shortcut. Issue commands like "Turn off the lights" or "Set the thermostat to 72 degrees."

Step 4: Automate Your Smart Home (Optional)

Enhance your innovative home experience by setting up automation:

- Create Scenes: Many intelligent home apps allow you to create scenes, which are predefined settings for multiple devices. For example, you could create a "Good Morning" scene that turns on lights and adjusts the thermostat with a single click.
- Set up Automation: Automation let you schedule actions or trigger events based on conditions. For instance, you can automate

your lights to turn on at sunset or receive a notification if a motion sensor detects movement.

- Explore Advanced Integrations (Optional): Some apps and services offer advanced integrations with other platforms, such as IFTTT (If This Then That) or HomeBridge, which can further extend the capabilities of your smart home setup.

Using Time Machine with External Drives

Step 1: Choose an External Drive

Before setting up Time Machine backups, you'll need an external drive with enough storage capacity to hold your backup data. Follow these steps to choose a suitable drive:

- Check Compatibility: Ensure the external drive is compatible with macOS and your MacBook Air. It should ideally have a USB, Thunderbolt, or USB-C connection.

- Sufficient Storage: Select a drive with ample storage space to accommodate your MacBook Air's data. Generally, the drive's capacity should be at least twice that of your laptop's internal storage.
- Format the Drive: If the external drive isn't already formatted in the macOS Extended (Journaled) format, you'll need to reformat it using Disk Utility. Make sure to back up any existing data on the drive before formatting.

Step 2: Configure Time Machine Backups

Now, let's set up Time Machine to start backing up your data:

- Open System Preferences: Click the Apple menu in the top-left corner of your screen, then select "System Preferences."
- Click on "Time Machine": In the System Preferences window, locate and click the "Time Machine" icon.
- Turn on Time Machine: Click the "On" button to enable Time Machine backups.

- Select Backup Disk: Click the "Select Disk" button to choose your external drive as the backup destination.
- Choose the Drive: Select your external drive in the list of available disks, then click the "Use Disk" button.
- Options (Optional): If you want to exclude specific files or folders from the backup, click the "Options" button. Add items to the exclusion list by clicking the "+" button.
- Start Backing Up: Once the external drive is selected, Time Machine will start the initial backup process; this may take some time, depending on how much data is backed up.

Step 3: Monitor and Manage Backups

After the initial setup, you can monitor and manage your Time Machine backups:

- Automatic Backups: Time Machine will automatically back up your data hourly, making it easy to recover files from various points in time.

- Backup Frequency (Optional): If you prefer less frequent backups, click the "Options" button in the Time Machine preferences to adjust the backup interval.
- Backup Now: To manually initiate a backup, click the Time Machine icon in the menu bar and select "Back Up Now."
- Restore Files: If you need to restore files, click the Time Machine icon, choose "Enter Time Machine," and navigate through the timeline to locate and restore specific files or folders.

Gaming with External Controllers

Step 1: Choose a Compatible Gaming Controller

Before you begin, ensure you have a compatible gaming controller for your MacBook Air 2023:

- Check Compatibility: Look for gaming controllers compatible with macOS and have drivers available. Popular options include

Xbox, PlayStation, and Nintendo Switch Pro controllers.

- Wired or Wireless: Decide whether you want a wired or wireless controller. Wireless controllers may require Bluetooth connectivity.
- Purchase and Unbox: Purchase the chosen gaming controller and unbox it. Ensure it comes with any necessary cables or adapters.

Step 2: Connect the Gaming Controller

Now, let's connect your gaming controller to your MacBook Air:

Wired Connection: If using a wired controller, connect it to your MacBook Air using the provided USB cable. Your MacBook should recognize the controller automatically.

- Wireless Connection: For wireless controllers:

a. Enable Bluetooth: On your MacBook Air, go to "System Preferences" > "Bluetooth" and ensure Bluetooth is turned on.

b. Put Controller in Pairing Mode: Press and hold the pairing button on the controller (refer to the controller's manual for instructions).

c. Pairing: Once the controller appears in the list of available devices on your MacBook, click "Connect" to pair them.

Step 3: Calibrate and Configure the Controller

After connecting the gaming controller, calibrate and configure it for optimal gaming performance:

- Open System Preferences: Click the Apple menu, then select "System Preferences."
- Click on "Controllers": In the System Preferences window, locate and click the "Controllers" icon.
- Calibrate the Controller: Select your connected gaming controller and click the "Calibrate" button. Follow the on-screen instructions to calibrate the controller's buttons and analog sticks.

- Test the Controller: Click the "Test" tab to ensure all buttons, triggers, and analog sticks work as expected. Make any necessary adjustments in the calibration settings.

Step 4: Configure the Controller in Games

Now that your gaming controller is connected and calibrated, you can configure it for specific games:

- Launch the Game: Open the game you want to play on your MacBook Air.
- Access Game Settings: Navigate to the game's settings or options menu.
- Controller Configuration: Look for a section related to controller settings. Games will often automatically detect and configure the connected gaming controller. Make any additional adjustments as needed.

Step 5: Enjoy Your Enhanced Gaming Experience

You're now ready to enjoy an enhanced gaming experience on your MacBook Air with the external gaming controller:

- Start Playing: Play your favorite games using the gaming controller's buttons, triggers, and analog sticks. Experience improved control and precision compared to using a keyboard and trackpad.
- Customize Controls (Optional): Some games allow you to customize button mappings and controls. Explore these options to tailor the gaming experience to your preferences.
- Disconnect the Controller: When you're done gaming, disconnect or turn the controller off.

Using Barcode Scanners

Barcode scanners can streamline inventory processes, minimize errors, and save time.

Step 1: Choose a Compatible Barcode Scanner

Before you begin, selecting a barcode scanner compatible with your MacBook Air 2023 is essential. Look for scanners that support USB or Bluetooth connectivity. Popular options include the Socket Mobile S700 or the TaoTronics TT-BS030.

Step 2: Connect the Barcode Scanner

- For USB Scanners:

a. Plug the USB cable of the scanner into an available USB port on your MacBook Air.

b. Your MacBook Air should automatically recognize the scanner. If not, visit the manufacturer's website to download any required drivers.

- For Bluetooth Scanners:

a. Turn on your scanner and put it in pairing mode according to the manufacturer's instructions.

b. On your MacBook Air, navigate to "System Preferences" > "Bluetooth."

c. Click "Turn Bluetooth On" if it's not already enabled.

d. Your scanner should appear in the list of available devices. Click on it to pair.

Step 3: Configure Scanner Settings

Open "System Preferences" on your MacBook Air.

Select "Keyboard" > "Shortcuts."

Click on "App Shortcuts" in the left sidebar.

Click the "+" button to add a new shortcut.

In the "Application" dropdown, choose the software you'll use with the barcode scanner (e.g., Excel, Google Sheets).

In the "Menu Title" field, type the exact name of the action you want to perform (e.g., "Paste").

Assign a unique keyboard shortcut, preferably one that doesn't conflict with existing shortcuts (e.g., Command + Option + Shift + V).

Step 4: Start Scanning

Open your preferred application for inventory management or data input.

Position the barcode scanner over the barcode and press the trigger button (or follow the scanner's instructions).

The scanner will capture the barcode and input the associated data into the active field of your application.

Step 5: Tips for Efficient Scanning

Ensure proper lighting conditions for accurate barcode reading.

Hold the scanner steady and at an appropriate distance from the barcode.

Regularly clean the scanner lens to prevent dust or smudges.

Keep a backup battery or charge the scanner to avoid interruptions.

Smart Card Readers

Smart card readers provide an added layer of security by requiring a physical card to verify your identity and grant access to sensitive information.

Step 1: Choose a Compatible Smart Card Reader

Look for readers that support USB or Bluetooth connectivity. Trusted options include the Gemalto IDBridge CT30 or the Identiv SCR3500.

Step 2: Connect the Smart Card Reader

- For USB Smart Card Readers:

a. Insert the USB connector of the smart card reader into an available USB port on your MacBook Air.

b. Your MacBook Air should recognize the card reader automatically.

- For Bluetooth Smart Card Readers:

a. Turn on your smart card reader and follow the manufacturer's instructions to put it in pairing mode.

b. On your MacBook Air, navigate to "System Preferences" > "Bluetooth."

c. Enable Bluetooth if it's not already turned on.

d. Locate your card reader in the list of available devices and click on it to pair.

Step 3: Install Required Software (if applicable)

Some smart card readers may require specific drivers or software for proper functionality. Visit the manufacturer's website to download and install the necessary drivers or applications.

Step 4: Insert and Authenticate with the Smart Card

Insert your smart card into the card reader.

Your MacBook Air may prompt you to enter a PIN or password associated with the smart card. Your organization or the card issuer typically provides this PIN.

Follow the on-screen instructions to complete the authentication process.

Step 5: Access Secure Systems and Data

Once authenticated, you can use your smart card to access secure systems, such as VPNs, encrypted email, or other authorized applications.

When prompted, insert your smart card into the reader to confirm your identity and gain access to the desired resource.

Step 6: Safely Remove the Smart Card

Before disconnecting the card or shutting down your MacBook Air 2023, ensure you safely remove the smart card:

Close any applications or systems that are using the smart card.

Eject the smart card from the reader through the operating system's eject mechanism (usually by clicking the eject icon next to the card's name).

Once ejected, you can safely remove the smart card from the reader.

Step 7: Tips for Secure Usage

Keep your smart card and reader in a secure location when not in use.

Memorize your PIN and never share it with anyone.

Regularly update your smart card's firmware and MacBook Air's software for the latest security enhancements.

Accessibility Devices

Switch Control is a powerful accessibility feature on macOS that allows users to control their MacBook Air using external switches. It's beneficial for individuals with limited mobility.

Step 1: Set Up Switch Control

Open "System Preferences" on your MacBook Air.

Go to "Accessibility" > "Switch Control."

Click "Enable Switch Control" to activate the feature.

Click "Switches" to configure how the switches will be used.

Step 2: Connect and Configure Switches

Connect external switches or compatible devices to available USB ports or Bluetooth switches.

In the "Switches" settings, add switches and assign actions (e.g., keystrokes, mouse clicks) to each button.

Step 3: Use the Switch Control

With Switch Control enabled, navigate menus and interact with elements by activating the switches as configured.

Customize dwell time (time required to activate a switch) and other settings to match your preferences.

Step 4: Braille Display Accessibility

Braille displays provide tactile output for visually impaired users, enabling them to read and interact with digital content.

Step 5: Connect a Braille Display

Connect a compatible USB or Bluetooth Braille display to your MacBook Air.

Open "System Preferences" > "Accessibility" > "VoiceOver."

Click "Braille" and select your Braille display from the list.

Step 6: Configure Braille Display Settings

Customize Braille display settings, including input, output, and display options.

Adjust verbosity settings to control the amount of Braille output.

Step 7: Experience Braille Accessibility

With VoiceOver enabled, navigate through macOS using the Braille display.

Read the text, interact with elements, and navigate the interface through tactile feedback.

Step 8: Additional Accessibility Features

Explore other accessibility features on MacBook Air, such as VoiceOver (screen reader), Zoom (magnification), and Display Accommodations (color and contrast adjustments).

Step 9: Stay Informed and Updated

Keep your MacBook Air's operating system and accessibility software up-to-date with the latest features and improvements.

CarPlay Integration

CarPlay is a feature that integrates your MacBook Air 2023 with your car's infotainment system, allowing you to safely interact with apps, make calls, send messages, and more while keeping your focus on the road.

Step 1: Check CarPlay Compatibility

Before you begin, ensure your car's infotainment system supports CarPlay.

Step 2: Connect MacBook Air to CarPlay

Start your car and connect your MacBook Air to your car's infotainment system using a USB cable.

The CarPlay interface may automatically appear on the infotainment screen, depending on your car model.

Step 3: Configure CarPlay Settings

On your car's infotainment screen, navigate to the CarPlay interface.

Use the touchscreen or vehicle controls to access the CarPlay settings.

Customize your CarPlay preferences, such as app arrangement, notifications, and Siri settings.

Step 4: Navigate Apps with CarPlay

Use the infotainment screen, touchscreen controls, or vehicle buttons to navigate the CarPlay interface.

Tap on app icons to launch and interact with apps like Apple Maps, Phone, Messages, Music, Podcasts, and more.

Step 5: Use Siri for Hands-Free Control

Activate Siri using the vehicle's voice control button or steering wheel controls.

Use voice commands to make calls, send messages, play music, and get directions without taking your hands off the wheel.

Step 6: Safely Access Messages and Calls

With CarPlay, you can access and respond to messages and calls using the infotainment system's controls or Siri.

Use voice commands to dictate messages and have incoming messages read aloud.

Step 7: Navigate with Apple Maps

Launch Apple Maps from the CarPlay interface.

Enter your destination using voice or touchscreen controls.

Follow turn-by-turn directions on the infotainment screen and listen to spoken instructions.

Step 8: Enjoy Music and Media

Access your music library, Apple Music, podcasts, and other media apps through CarPlay.

Control playback using the infotainment system's controls or Siri.

Step 9: Disconnect and Exit CarPlay

Safely disconnect your MacBook Air from the car's infotainment system by unplugging the USB cable.

The CarPlay interface should automatically exit, or you can navigate away from it on the infotainment screen.

Step 10: Drive Safely

While CarPlay enhances convenience, remember that safety is a top priority. Focus on driving and use hands-free features whenever possible.

CHAPTER SEVEN

Advanced Audio Routing

Regarding professional audio production and mixing, advanced audio routing techniques can significantly enhance your workflow and creative opportunities. Here are some advanced techniques that experienced audio engineers and producers often use to achieve exceptional results:

- **Aggregate Audio Devices**

Combine multiple audio interfaces (if available) to increase the number of inputs and outputs for recording and routing within your DAW. macOS allows you to create an aggregate audio device to utilize multiple interfaces simultaneously.

- **Virtual Mixer Routing**

Utilize virtual mixers or internal routing plugins within your DAW (Digital Audio Workstation) to create complex signal paths; this can be particularly useful for parallel processing, subgrouping, or routing signals to various effects chains.

- **Auxiliary Tracks for Parallel Processing**

Set up auxiliary tracks in your DAW and route multiple channels to them. Apply effects like reverb, delay, or saturation to these aux tracks, blending them into the mix; this allows for consistent and controlled results across multiple channels.

- **Advanced Sidechain Compression**

Utilize sidechain compression creatively by routing different audio sources to trigger reduction on specific tracks; this can be used for intricate rhythmic effects, dynamic control, and frequency shaping.

- **Advanced Panning and Binaural Mixing**

Experiment with advanced panning techniques to create immersive soundscapes. Use binaural panning plugins to simulate 3D audio experiences, enhancing spatial depth and realism.

- **Bus Processing for Mastering**

Set up bus processing for mastering purposes. Route all tracks through a bus where you can apply mastering-grade EQ, compression, and limiting to shape the final mix.

- **Feedback Loops for Sound Design**

Create feedback loops by routing the output of a track back into its input. Apply effects, modulation, and automation to generate evolving and experimental sound textures.

- **Advanced MIDI Routing**

Utilize MIDI routing to control multiple instruments and effects simultaneously. Use MIDI effects to create intricate sequences and modulations.

- **Dynamic EQ and Multiband Compression**

Apply dynamic EQ or multiband compression to specific frequency bands of a track, allowing surgical control over the mix and helping address frequency masking issues.

- **Parallel Multiband Processing**

Set up parallel processing for different frequency bands. Route a track through multiple chains with additional processing for each frequency range, then mix them back together.

- **External Hardware Integration**

If you have external hardware processors or synthesizers, use your MacBook Air's audio interface to route audio to and from these devices, integrating them into your mix.

- **Automated Sends for Creative Effects**

Automate send levels to effects like reverb, delay, or granular processors; this can create dynamic and evolving soundscapes over time.

Remember to always keep backups of your projects before experimenting with advanced routing, and take note of what works best for your specific projects and creative preferences. The MacBook Air's portability and processing power make it a versatile tool for implementing these advanced techniques in your professional audio production and mixing workflow.

Network Attached Storage (NAS)

A NAS provides centralized storage and file-sharing capabilities over a network, allowing you to access, organize, and manage your files seamlessly.

Step 1: Set Up Your NAS Device

Follow the manufacturer's instructions to set up and configure your NAS device on your local network.

Ensure the NAS is powered on, connected to your network, and accessible.

Step 2: Locate NAS Device IP Address

Log in to your router's web interface using a web browser.

Find the connected devices or DHCP client list section to locate the IP address assigned to your NAS device.

Step 3: Connect to the NAS from MacBook Air

Open Finder on your MacBook Air.

In the menu bar, click "Go" > "Connect to Server" (or press Command + K).

Enter the NAS device's IP address using the following format: smb://NAS_IP_ADDRESS (replace NAS_IP_ADDRESS with the actual IP address).

Click "Connect."

Step 4: Provide Credentials

If prompted, enter the username and password you set up for accessing the NAS device.

Choose the option to remember the credentials in your keychain for automatic access in the future.

Step 5: Access and Manage Files

Once connected, you'll see the NAS device listed in Finder's sidebar.

Browse through the shared folders on the NAS, similar to navigating your local files.

Open, copy, move, or delete files on the NAS as you would with local files.

Step 6: Mount NAS as Drive (Optional)

To access the NAS more conveniently, you can mount it as a network drive on your MacBook Air.

In Finder, click "Finder" > "Preferences."

In the "Sidebar" tab, check the box next to your NAS device under "Shared" to have it appear in the Finder sidebar.

Also, you can drag the NAS icon from the Finder window to the desktop for quick access.

Step 7: Collaborative File Sharing (Optional)

Set up shared folders on the NAS for collaborative projects.

Share access to specific folders with other users on your network, allowing them to access, edit, and manage files.

Step 8: Backup and Sync (Optional)

Consider using backup and sync software to automatically back up files from your MacBook Air to the NAS, ensuring data redundancy.

Step 9: Disconnect from the NAS

To disconnect from the NAS, eject the mounted drive or click the "Disconnect" button next to the NAS device in Finder's sidebar.

External Scanner Integration

External scanners provide a reliable way to digitize physical documents, enabling you to create digital copies and organize your paperwork.

Step 1: Choose a Compatible Scanner

Before you begin, select an external scanner that is compatible with macOS. Look for scanners that offer USB or wireless connectivity options.

Step 2: Connect the Scanner

- For USB Scanners:

a. Plug the USB cable of the scanner into an available USB port on your MacBook Air.

b. Your MacBook Air should automatically recognize the scanner.

- For Wireless Scanners:

a. Follow the manufacturer's instructions to connect the scanner to your Wi-Fi network.

b. Download any necessary software or apps provided by the scanner manufacturer.

Step 3: Install Scanner Software (if applicable)

Some scanners may require installing specific software or drivers on your MacBook Air. Follow the manufacturer's instructions to install the software needed.

Step 4: Place the Document and Configure Settings

Lift the scanner lid or open the document feeder, depending on the type of scanner.

Place the document you want to scan face down on the scanner glass or in the document feeder.

Use the scanner's control panel or software on your MacBook Air to configure scanning settings such as resolution, color mode, file format, and destination folder.

Step 5: Initiate Scanning

On your MacBook Air, open the scanner software or application that came with the scanner (if applicable).

Select the type of scan you want to perform (e.g., color, black and white, grayscale).

Click the "Scan" or "Start" button to initiate the scanning process.

Step 6: Review and Edit Scanned Documents

After scanning, review the scanned document on your MacBook Air's screen.

Use built-in software or third-party applications to edit, crop, rotate, or enhance the scanned document.

Step 7: Save and Organize Scanned Documents

Choose a location on your MacBook Air where you want to save the scanned document.

Rename the file if necessary, and select the desired format (e.g., PDF, JPEG).

Organize scanned documents into folders for easy retrieval.

Step 8: Eject or Turn Off the Scanner

After scanning, safely eject the scanner from your MacBook Air or turn off the scanner, depending on the manufacturer's recommendations.

Step 9: Advanced Features (Optional)

Explore advanced scanner software features, such as optical character recognition (OCR), for converting scanned text into editable documents.

Custom Device Profiles

Custom device profiles allow you to tailor your system to specific tasks, ensuring the best performance, battery life, and user experience.

Step 1: Understand Custom Device Profiles

Custom device profiles adjust system settings to suit specific use cases. They can optimize performance, battery life, or other parameters based on your preferences.

Step 2: Identify Usage Scenarios

Determine different scenarios in which you use your MacBook Air. For example, you might create profiles for work, gaming, video editing, or extended battery life.

Step 3: Create a Custom Profile

Click the Apple logo in the top-left corner of the screen and choose "System Preferences."

Select "Energy Saver" or "Battery" (depending on your macOS version) and click the "Schedule" button.

Click the checkbox next to "Start up or wake" and set the time for your custom profile.

Adjust screen brightness, display sleep, and system sleep duration to match your usage scenario.

Click "OK" to save the custom profile.

Step 4: Name and Save the Profile

Click the "Battery" icon in the menu bar.

Select "Battery Preferences."

Click the "+" button to create a new profile.

Name the profile based on the scenario (e.g., "High Performance," "Long Battery Life," "Video Editing").

Adjust settings such as display brightness, keyboard backlight, and more to match the scenario's requirements.

Click "Create."

Step 5: Switch Between Profiles

Click the "Battery" icon in the menu bar.

Select the profile you want to switch to from the dropdown menu.

Your MacBook Air will adjust settings according to the selected profile.

Step 6: Manage Profiles

To manage existing profiles, go to "System Preferences" > "Energy Saver" or "Battery" and click the "Battery Preferences" button.

Edit, duplicate, or delete profiles as needed.

Step 7: Automate Profile Switching (Optional)

You can use third-party apps like "Scenario" or "Alfred" to automate profile switching based on conditions like time of day or connected peripherals.

Step 8: Review and Adjust

Review and adjust your custom profiles periodically based on changing usage patterns or preferences.

Consider creating profiles for new scenarios you encounter.

Device Management and Device Management Software

Device management involves controlling and monitoring multiple devices to ensure proper functionality, security, and compliance. It requires configuration, software deployment, updates, security policies enforcement, and remote troubleshooting.

Benefits of Device Management

Efficiency: Streamline device setup, configuration, and maintenance processes.

Security: Enforce security policies, monitor device health, and apply security patches remotely.

Consistency: Maintain consistent settings and configurations across multiple devices.

Remote Management: Diagnose and troubleshoot issues remotely, reducing downtime.

Software Deployment: Install, update, and manage applications on multiple devices simultaneously.

Device Management Software

- Apple Configurator 2:

Apple Configurator 2 is a macOS application that allows you to configure and manage multiple iOS and macOS devices, including your MacBook Air. It provides features such as device provisioning, app deployment, and configuration profile management.

- Mobile Device Management (MDM) Solutions:

MDM solutions are designed to manage and secure mobile devices, including laptops like the MacBook Air. These solutions offer features like remote device enrollment, configuration, app deployment, security policies enforcement, and remote wiping.

- Notable MDM solutions include:

Jamf Pro: It's a comprehensive MDM solution for Apple devices that offers advanced device management, security features, and automation.

Fleetsmith: A cloud-based MDM platform that simplifies device management for Apple devices.

Mosyle Manager: Offers a user-friendly MDM solution with features like app deployment, remote commands, and classroom management.

- Third-Party Device Management Tools:

Some third-party tools provide cross-platform device management, enabling you to manage macOS and non-Apple devices from a single interface. Examples include:

Microsoft Intune: A cloud-based endpoint management solution for Windows, macOS, iOS, and Android devices.

VMware Workspace ONE: Offers unified endpoint management for diverse device types, including macOS.

CHAPTER EIGHT

App Store Access

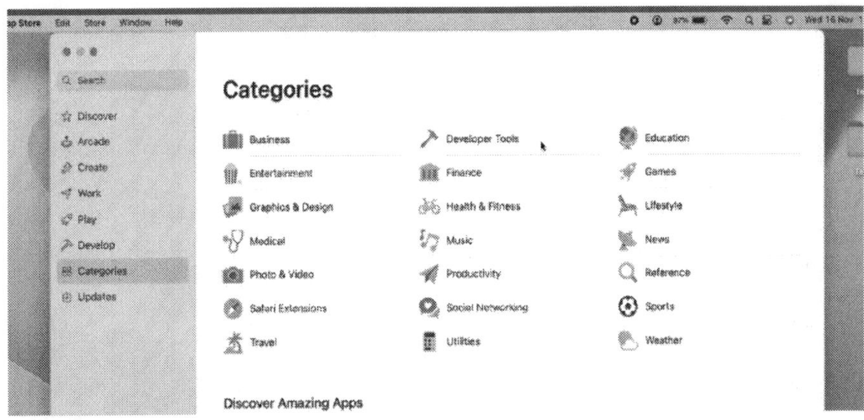

The App Store is a fantastic resource for discovering and downloading a wide range of apps to enhance your experience with your MacBook Air 2023.

Step 1: Accessing the App Store

Click on the "Launchpad" icon located in your Dock. This icon looks like a gray rocket ship.

In the Launchpad, locate and click on the "App Store" icon. It resembles a blue "A" symbol.

The App Store will now open, and you'll be greeted with the homepage showcasing featured apps and categories.

Step 2: Navigating the App Store

Search Bar: You'll see a search bar at the top-right corner of the App Store. Use this to search for specific apps. Type in the name of the app you're looking for and press "Return" on your keyboard.

Categories: To explore apps by categories, look to the left-hand side of the App Store window. Click on a category (e.g., "Productivity," "Games," "Utilities") to see a curated list of apps in that category.

Featured: The "Featured" tab at the top-left corner highlights recommended apps and collections. Explore these selections to discover popular and well-reviewed apps.

Top Charts: Click "Top Charts" to see the most popular apps based on downloads and ratings. You can choose between "Free" and "Paid" apps.

Updates: Click on the "Updates" tab to keep your apps up-to-date. Here, you'll find pending app updates that you can install simultaneously.

Step 3: Downloading and Installing Apps

After finding an app you want to download, click on its icon to open its details page.

You'll see a "Get" or "Download" button on the app's details page. Click on it.

If prompted, enter your Apple ID and password. This step ensures that you're authorized to download apps.

The app will start downloading, and its icon will appear in the "Launchpad" once the download is complete.

Tips and Reminders:

- Keep your Apple ID credentials secure and avoid sharing them.

- Some apps are free, while others require a purchase. Make sure you understand the app's pricing before proceeding.
- If you encounter app downloads or installation issues, check your internet connection and ensure your MacBook Air's software is current.

Installing and Uninstalling Apps

Step 1: Installing Apps from the App Store

Access the App Store by following the steps outlined in the previous guide.

Search for the app you want to install using the search bar or browse through categories, featured apps, or top charts.

Once you've found the app you want, click on its icon to open its details page.

On the app's details page, locate the "Get" or "Download" button and click on it.

If prompted, enter your Apple ID and password to authorize the download.

The app will start downloading, and its icon will appear in the "Launchpad" once the download is complete.

Step 2: Uninstalling Apps from your MacBook Air

Locate the app you want to uninstall in your "Launchpad" or "Applications" folder. If the app is in the Launchpad, click and hold its icon until it starts to wiggle.

Once the icons are wiggling, you'll see a small "X" icon in the corner of each app. Click the "X" icon on the app you want to uninstall.

A confirmation dialog will appear, asking if you want to delete the app. Click "Delete" to confirm.

The app will be uninstalled from your MacBook Air 2023, and its icon will disappear from the "Launchpad" or "Applications" folder.

Updating Apps

Regularly updating your apps ensures access to the latest features, improvements, and bug fixes.

Step 1: Checking for App Updates

Open the App Store on your MacBook Air 2023 by following the steps outlined in our previous guide.

In the App Store, click on the "Updates" tab at the top of the window.

You'll see a list of available updates for your installed apps. Apps with pending updates will have an "Update" button next to their names.

Step 2: Updating Apps from the App Store

To update all your apps immediately, click the "Update All" button at the top-right corner of the "Updates" tab.

If you prefer updating individual apps, click the "Update" button next to each.

If prompted, enter your Apple ID and password to authorize the updates.

The updates will begin downloading and installing. You can monitor the progress in the "Updates" tab.

Step 3: Automatic App Updates (Optional)

You can enable automatic app updates on your MacBook Air to streamline the process.

Click the "Apple" menu at the top-left corner of your screen and select "System Preferences."

Choose "App Store" from the System Preferences window.

Check the box next to "Automatically check for updates" and "Download newly available updates in the background."

With automatic updates enabled, your apps will be updated silently in the background, ensuring you always have the latest versions.

Managing App Permissions

App permissions allow you to control which resources an app can access, such as your camera, microphone, and location. By managing app permissions, you can enhance your privacy and security while using your MacBook Air 2023.

Step 1: Accessing App Permissions

Click the "Apple" menu at the top-left corner of your screen and select "System Preferences."

In the System Preferences window, click on "Security & Privacy."

Navigate to the "Privacy" tab at the top of the Security & Privacy window.

Step 2: Managing App Permissions

In the Privacy tab, you'll see a list of resource categories on the left (e.g., Camera, Microphone, Location Services). Click on a category to manage permissions for that resource.

- To grant permissions to an app:

a. Click the lock icon at the bottom-left corner of the window and enter your administrator password if prompted.

b. Check the box next to the app you want to grant access to, allowing the app to use the selected resource.

- To revoke permissions from an app:

a. Click the lock icon and enter your administrator password if needed.

b. Uncheck the box next to the app you want to revoke access to; this will prevent the app from using the selected resource.

Step 3: Customizing App Permissions (Optional)

Some apps may prompt you for permission the first time they try to access a resource. You can customize these permissions by clicking the "Details" button next to the resource category.

In the Details view, you'll see a list of apps and their corresponding permissions for that resource. Adjust permissions by checking or unchecking the boxes next to each app.

Tips and Reminders:

- Be cautious when granting permissions. Only give access to resources that are necessary for the app's functionality.
- Review and update app permissions periodically to ensure your privacy preferences are current.
- If you're unsure about an app's permissions, consider researching the app's purpose and reading user reviews before granting access.

Using Pre-installed Apps

Your MacBook Air 2023 has various built-in apps to enhance productivity, communication, and organization.

App 1: Safari - Your Web Browsing Companion

Safari is your default web browser on your MacBook Air. Here's how to use it effectively:

Step 1: Browsing the Web

Click on the "Safari" icon in your Dock or use Spotlight search (Command + Spacebar) to open Safari.

Enter a web address or search term in the address bar and press "Return" to load a website.

Use tabs to keep multiple web pages open simultaneously. Click the "+" button on the tab bar to open a new one.

App 2: Mail - Managing Your Email

Mail helps you manage your emails in one place. Here's how to get started:

Step 1: Setting Up Email Accounts

Open "Mail" from the Dock or Applications folder.

Follow the on-screen prompts to add your email accounts. Enter your email address and password, and Mail will automatically configure settings for popular email services.

Step 2: Composing and Sending Emails

Click the "Compose" button (pencil icon) to create a new email.

Enter the recipient's email address, subject, and message.

Click "Send" to deliver your email.

App 3: Calendar - Organizing Your Schedule

Calendar helps you keep track of appointments, events, and more. Here's how to use it effectively:

Step 1: Adding Events

Open "Calendar" from the Dock or Applications folder.

Click the "+" button to add a new event.

Enter event details such as title, location, date, and time.

Click "Add" to save the event to your calendar.

App 4: Notes - Capturing Your Thoughts

Notes are your digital notebook for jotting ideas, lists, and more. Here's how to use it:

Step 1: Creating Notes

Open "Notes" from the Dock or Applications folder.

Click the "+" button to create a new note.

Type or paste your text into the note. You can also add images, links, and checklists.

Click outside the note to save your changes.

- Additional Essential Apps:

Contacts: Manage your contacts, phone numbers, and addresses in one place.

Messages: Stay in touch with friends and family through instant messaging.

FaceTime: Make video and audio calls to other Apple devices.

Tips and Reminders:

- Explore the menus and options within each app to discover more features.
- Sync your apps with iCloud to access your data across multiple devices.

Customizing App Preferences

By customizing settings and preferences for individual apps, you can tailor them to match your personal preferences and optimize your user experience.

Step 1: Accessing App Preferences

Launch the app you want to customize preferences for. For example, let's use Safari.

Click on the "Safari" menu in the screen's top-left corner, next to the Apple logo.

From the dropdown menu, select "Preferences."

Step 2: Customizing App Preferences

You'll find multiple tabs representing different settings categories in the Preferences window for the selected app (e.g., Safari).

Explore each tab to customize various aspects of the app. For Safari, you can customize settings such as the homepage, default search engine, privacy preferences, and more.

Adjust settings according to your preferences. For instance, you can set your homepage to a specific website, turn pop-up blocking on/off, and choose your preferred search engine.

Step 3: Applying Changes

Once you've customized your settings, click the "Close" button to exit the Preferences window.

Your changes will be applied immediately, and the app will reflect your personalized preferences.

Tips and Reminders:

- Each app has its own set of preferences and settings. Explore the preferences menu of individual apps to discover customization options.
- Some apps may have advanced settings that can significantly affect their functionality. Be cautious while making changes to avoid unintended consequences.

Organizing Apps in Folders

Organizing your apps into folders can help you declutter your desktop or Launchpad, making it easier to find and access your apps.

Step 1: Creating an App Folder

Start by selecting the apps you want to group in a folder. You can choose apps with similar purposes or functions.

Click and hold on to one of the selected apps.

Drag the app on top of another selected app. As you do this, a folder will automatically be created, and the two apps will be placed inside the folder.

Release the mouse button to create the folder.

Step 2: Renaming the App Folder

After creating the folder, it will have a default name based on the category of apps you grouped.

Click once on the folder to select it, then click on its name to highlight it.

Type in the desired name for the folder and press "Return" to save the new name.

Step 3: Managing App Folders

To open an app folder, double-click on it, revealing the apps contained within the folder.

To add more apps to a folder, drag and drop them onto the folder icon.

To remove apps from a folder, click and hold the app you want to remove, drag it out of the folder, and release the mouse button.

To delete an app folder, drag all the apps out. The folder will automatically be deleted.

Step 4: Organizing in Launchpad

You can also create and manage app folders in the Launchpad for a more organized layout.

Open the Launchpad by clicking on the "Launchpad" icon in your Dock.

Click and hold on an app icon until the icons start to wiggle.

Drag an app onto another app to create a folder. Follow the same steps as creating a folder on the desktop.

Tips and Reminders:

- Organize your apps in a way that makes sense to you, such as grouping by purpose, frequency of use, or type.
- To keep things organized, consider creating folders for specific projects, hobbies, or work-related tasks.

Spotlight Search for Apps

Spotlight is a powerful built-in search feature that lets you quickly locate and access apps, files, and more on your device.

Step 1: Accessing Spotlight Search

To open Spotlight search, press the "Command" key (⌘) and the "Spacebar" simultaneously. Alternatively, click the magnifying glass icon in the top-right corner of your screen.

A search bar and the Spotlight search window will appear at the center of your screen.

Step 2: Searching for Apps

In the Spotlight search bar, begin typing the name of the app you want to open. As you do this, Spotlight will start displaying search results in real-time.

The search results will automatically update as you type to match your input. You'll see a list of suggested apps, documents, and other relevant items.

Use the arrow keys on your keyboard to navigate the search results and highlight the app you want to open.

Step 3: Opening the App

Once the desired app is highlighted, press "Return" on your keyboard to open the app immediately.

Alternatively, you can click on the app's icon in the Spotlight search window to open it.

Step 4: Additional Actions

If the app you're looking for doesn't appear in the initial search results, press "Return" to see more results in the Spotlight search window.

You can also use Spotlight search to perform other tasks, such as searching for files, searching the web, performing calculations, and more. Just type your query in the search bar to see relevant results.

Tips and Reminders:

- Spotlight search is a versatile tool that can save you time by quickly accessing apps and performing various tasks.
- You can use natural language queries in Spotlight. For example, type "Weather in New York" or "Define effervescent" to get instant results.

Full-Screen and Split-Screen Modes

These modes allow you to maximize your screen real estate by optimizing your app layout.

- Full-Screen Mode

Full-screen mode allows you to dedicate your entire screen to a single app, eliminating distractions and maximizing focus.

Step 1: Entering Full-Screen Mode

Open the app you want to use in full-screen mode.

Click the green "Full Screen" button at the app window's top-left corner. Alternatively, press the "Control" key (^) and the "Command" key (⌘) along with the "F" key simultaneously.

Step 2: Exiting Full-Screen Mode

Move your cursor to the top of the screen to reveal the menu bar.

Click the green "Exit Full Screen" button at the top-left corner. Alternatively, press the "Control" key (^) and the "Command" key (⌘) along with the "F" key again.

- Split-Screen Mode

Split-screen mode allows you to work with two apps, enhancing your multitasking capabilities.

Step 1: Entering Split-Screen Mode

Open the first app you want to use in split-screen mode.

Click and hold the green "Full Screen" button at the top-left corner of the app window.

Drag the app to the left or right edge of the screen until a blue outline appears.

Release the mouse button to snap the app to that side of the screen.

Choose the second app you want to use from the other open apps or the Dock. The second app will automatically snap to the opposite side.

Step 2: Adjusting Split-Screen Layout

Move the divider between the two apps to adjust each app's space.

To switch the positions of the apps, click and hold the title bar of one app, then drag it to the opposite side.

Step 3: Exiting Split-Screen Mode

Move your cursor to the top of the screen to reveal the menu bar.

Click the green "Exit Full Screen" button to exit split-screen mode on one of the apps.

Tips and Reminders:

- Experiment with different apps to find the most effective split-screen combinations for your workflow.
- Use gestures on the trackpad (swipe left/right with four fingers) to quickly switch between full-screen apps.

App Switcher and Force Quit

The App Switcher lets you quickly switch between open apps without minimizing or closing them.

Step 1: Accessing the App Switcher

To open the App Switcher, press the "Command" (⌘) key along with the "Tab" key. A row of app icons will appear in the center of the screen.

While holding down the "Command" key, press the "Tab" key repeatedly to cycle through the open apps. Release both keys to switch to the selected app.

Step 2: Navigating the App Switcher

With the App Switcher open, you can use the arrow keys to navigate through the app icons.

To select an app, release the "Command" key to switch to that app.

You can also use the trackpad to swipe left or right with three or four fingers to navigate the open apps.

- Force Quitting Unresponsive Apps

Force quitting is used when an app becomes unresponsive or freezes.

Step 1: Accessing Force Quit Applications

Click on the "Apple" menu at the top-left corner of the screen and select "Force Quit."

Or, you can press the "Option" (⌥), "Command" (⌘), and "Esc" keys simultaneously.

Step 2: Force Quitting an App

You'll see a list of open apps in the Force Quit Applications window.

Select the unresponsive app from the list.

Click the "Force Quit" button at the window's bottom-right corner.

Confirm your choice by clicking "Force Quit" in the confirmation dialog.

Tips and Reminders:

- The App Switcher is a quick way to switch between running apps without returning to the desktop or Dock.
- Force quitting should be a last resort. Try closing the app usually or using the App Switcher before resorting to force quitting.

Widgets in macOS

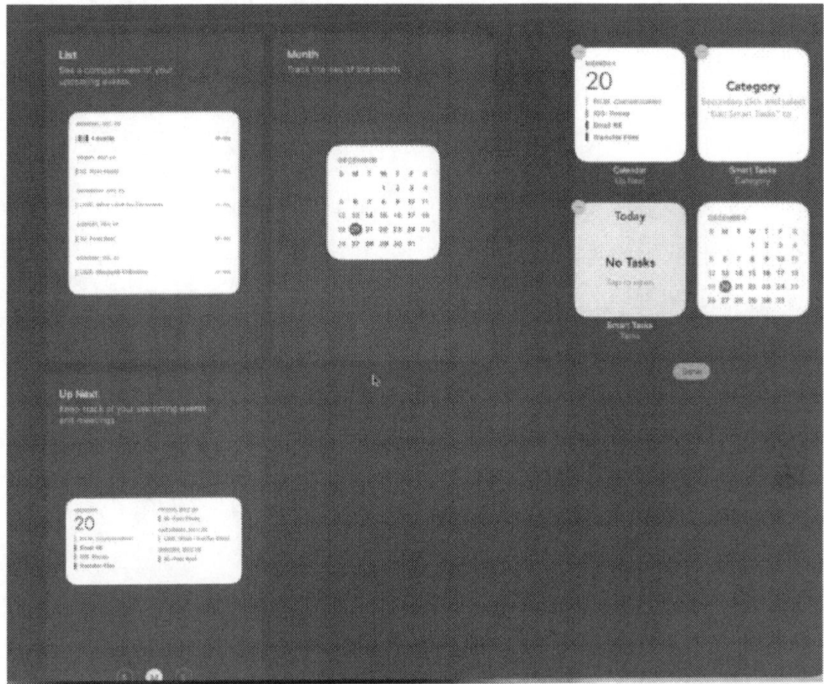

Widgets provide a convenient way to access app information and functionality without fully opening the apps.

Step 1: Accessing the Today View

Click the "Today View" icon at the menu bar's top-right corner. It looks like a circle with a vertical line through it.

You can also use the "Notification Center" gesture on your trackpad (swipe left with two fingers from the right edge of the trackpad) to open the Today View.

Step 2: Adding and Removing Widgets

In the Today View, you'll see a variety of widgets available for customization.

To add a widget, scroll down to the bottom of the Today View and click the "Edit" button.

A list of available widgets will appear. Click the "+" button next to anyone to add it to your Today View.

To remove a widget, click the red "-" button next to the widget's name in the Edit Widgets list.

Step 3: Rearranging Widgets

In the Edit Widgets list, you can rearrange the order of widgets by clicking and dragging the handle icon (three horizontal lines) next to a widget's name.

Drag the widget to the desired position in the list.

Step 4: Using Widgets

Once you've customized your Today View with widgets, you can interact with them directly.

Click on a widget to expand or interact with its content. For example, you can view weather information, calendar events, news headlines, and more.

Some widgets may provide interactive elements, such as buttons or links, that allow you to perform actions without opening the respective app.

Step 5: Customizing Widget Preferences (Optional)

Some widgets may offer customization options. To access these options, click the "Customize" button within the widget.

Adjust settings or select preferences according to your needs.

Tips and Reminders:

- Experiment with different widgets to find the most useful for your daily tasks.
- Widgets can provide at-a-glance information and quick access to app functionality, enhancing productivity.

CHAPTER NINE

Using Productivity Apps

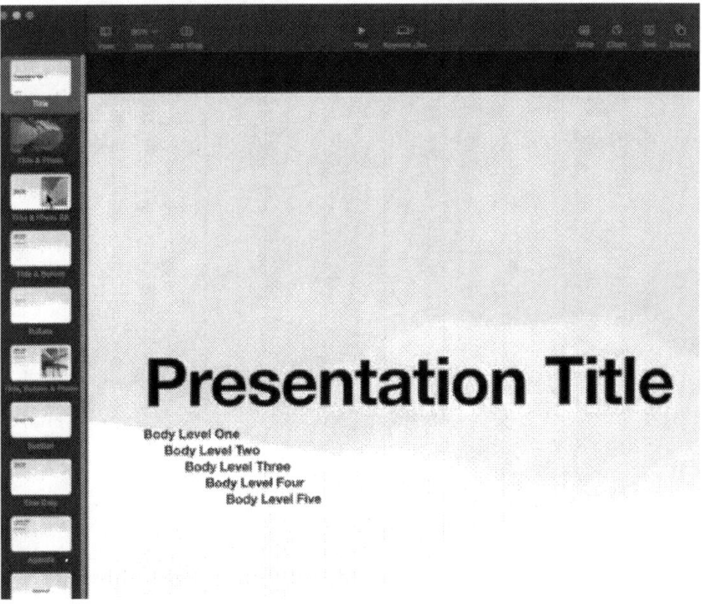

Productivity apps like Freeform, Keynote, Numbers, and Pages offer powerful tools for creating, editing, and collaborating on documents, presentations, spreadsheets, and more.

App 1: Freeform - Creative Document Editing

Freeform is a versatile app that allows you to create visually engaging documents with text, images, and more.

Step 1: Creating a Document

Open Freeform from the Applications folder or Launchpad.

Click the "+" button to create a new document.

Use the tools and options to add text, images, shapes, and other elements to your document.

App 2: Keynote - Dynamic Presentations

Keynote lets you create captivating presentations for various purposes.

Step 1: Creating a Presentation

Open Keynote from the Applications folder or Launchpad.

Click the "+" button to start a new presentation.

Choose a template or start with a blank slide.

App 3: Numbers - Effective Spreadsheet Management

Numbers allow you to create and manage spreadsheets with ease.

Step 1: Create a Spreadsheet

Open Numbers from the Applications folder or Launchpad.

Click the "+" button to create a new spreadsheet.

Use the built-in tools to add data, create formulas, and design charts.

App 4: Pages - Professional Document Creation

Pages offer comprehensive tools for creating beautifully formatted documents.

Step 1: Creating a Document

Open Pages from the Applications folder or Launchpad.

Click the "+" button to start a new document.

Choose a template or start with a blank page.

Collaboration Tips:

- iCloud: Use iCloud to collaborate on documents with others in real-time. Share documents and allow others to view or edit them.
- Comments and Annotations: Add comments and annotations to provide feedback and suggestions to collaborators.
- Version History: Track changes and access previous versions of a document using the version history feature.

Tips and Reminders:

- Familiarize yourself with keyboard shortcuts to work more efficiently in these apps.
- Explore the app menus and toolbars to discover additional features and options.

Creative Apps for Media Editing

Creative apps such as Adobe Creative Suite, iMovie, and GarageBand offer a wide range of tools for editing photos, videos, and audio, allowing you to bring your artistic visions to life.

App 1: Adobe Creative Suite - Professional Creative Suite

Adobe Creative Suite includes applications like Adobe Photoshop, Illustrator, and Premiere Pro for comprehensive media editing.

Step 1: Media Editing

Open the desired Adobe Creative Suite app from your Applications folder or Launchpad.

Import your media (photos, videos, graphics) into the app.

Use extensive tools to edit and enhance your media content.

App 2: iMovie - Video Editing Made Easy

iMovie offers user-friendly tools for editing and creating impressive videos.

Step 1: Importing Media

Open iMovie from your Applications folder or Launchpad.

Create a new project and import video clips, images, and audio.

Step 2: Editing and Enhancing

Drag and drop media onto the timeline to arrange your task.

Trim, split, and set clips for smooth transitions.

Add transitions, effects, titles, and soundtracks to enhance your video.

App 3: GarageBand - Audio Editing and Music Creation

GarageBand lets you create and edit audio tracks and music compositions.

Step 1: Creating a Project

Open GarageBand from your Applications folder or Launchpad.

Choose a project template (e.g., songwriting, podcast, voice recording).

Step 2: Editing and Recording

Add audio recordings, loops, and virtual instruments to your project.

Edit audio tracks, adjust volume, add effects, and arrange the composition.

Tips:

- Practice and Tutorials: Explore tutorials and practice with the apps to unlock their full potential.
- Presets and Templates: Use presets and templates to jumpstart your creative projects.
- Export and Sharing: Learn to export your creations in various formats and share them with others.

Entertainment Apps

Your MacBook Air is versatile for entertainment, offering a variety of apps to keep you entertained and engaged.

App 1: Music Streaming - Spotify

Spotify offers a vast library of music tracks, albums, and playlists for streaming.

Step 1: Accessing Spotify

Open your web browser, visit the Spotify website, or download the Spotify app from the Mac App Store.

Sign up for a free account or log in if you already have one.

Step 2: Exploring Music

Search for your favorite artists, albums, or songs using the search bar.

Create and follow playlists, discover new music, and enjoy personalized recommendations.

App 2: Video Streaming - Netflix

Netflix provides a wide range of TV shows, movies, and original content for streaming.

Step 1: Accessing Netflix

Open your web browser and visit the Netflix website or download the Netflix app from the Mac App Store.

Sign up for an account or log in if you have one.

Step 2: Browsing and Watching

Browse categories, genres, and recommendations to find the content you want.

Click on a title to start streaming.

App 3: Gaming - Steam

Steam is a popular platform for purchasing and playing various video games.

Step 1: Accessing Steam

Download and install the Steam app from the official website.

Create a Steam account or log in if you have one.

Step 2: Exploring and Playing Games

Browse the Steam store for games across different genres.

Purchase and download games to your library, then launch and play them.

App 4: Reading - Apple Books

Apple Books offers many e-books and audiobooks for reading and listening.

Step 1: Accessing Apple Books

Open the Apple Books app, which is pre-installed on your MacBook Air.

Sign in with your Apple ID or create one if needed.

Step 2: Browsing and Reading

Browse the store for e-books and audiobooks in various genres.

Purchase or download titles to your library and start reading.

Tips:

- Subscription Services: Consider subscribing to premium services for ad-free and enhanced experiences.
- Discover Content: Explore categories, genres, and recommendations to discover new entertainment.

Productivity Extensions

App extensions and plugins are powerful tools that can expand the capabilities of your favorite apps, making them even more valuable and efficient.

App Extension 1: Grammarly - Writing Assistant

Grammarly is a writing assistant that helps you enhance your writing quality and correctness.

Step 1: Installing Grammarly

Visit the Grammarly website or download the Grammarly extension from the Mac App Store.

Install the extension and sign up for a Grammarly account.

Step 2: Using Grammarly

Grammarly will automatically check your spelling, grammar, and punctuation as you type in supported apps.

Click on underlined errors to see suggestions and corrections.

App Extension 2: Evernote Web Clipper - Note-Taking and Organization

Evernote Web Clipper allows you to save and organize web content for later use.

Step 1: Installing Evernote Web Clipper

Visit the Evernote website or download the Evernote Web Clipper extension from the Mac App Store.

Install the extension and sign in with your Evernote account.

Step 2: Clipping Web Content

Use the Evernote Web Clipper icon in your browser's toolbar to clip articles, images, and more from the web.

Choose a notebook and add tags to organize your clips.

App Plugin 1: Adobe Stock - Creative Assets

Adobe Stock provides access to high-quality images and assets directly within compatible apps.

Step 1: Accessing Adobe Stock

Open a compatible Adobe app such as Photoshop or Illustrator.

Navigate to the Libraries panel and click on "Adobe Stock."

Step 2: Browsing and Using Assets

Search for images, illustrations, videos, and more within Adobe Stock.

License and use the assets directly within your Adobe project.

App Plugin 2: Trello for Chrome - Task Management

Trello for Chrome is a browser plugin that integrates Trello's task management features into your web browser.

Step 1: Adding Trello for Chrome

Visit the Chrome Web Store and search for "Trello for Chrome."

Install the extension and sign in with your Trello account.

Step 2: Accessing Trello

Click on the Trello icon in your browser's toolbar to access your Trello boards and tasks.

Manage and update tasks directly from your browser.

Tips:

- Customization: Explore settings and options within extensions/plugins to personalize their behavior.
- Compatibility: Ensure the extensions/plugins are compatible with your apps and browser.

Security Apps

Security apps protect your device and personal information from potential threats.

App 1: Malwarebytes - Malware Protection

Malwarebytes is a powerful anti-malware tool that helps detect and remove malicious software.

Step 1: Installing Malwarebytes

Visit the Malwarebytes website or download the Malwarebytes app from the Mac App Store.

Install the app and follow the on-screen instructions to set up your account.

Step 2: Scanning for Malware

Open Malwarebytes and click the "Scan" button to initiate a system scan.

Malwarebytes will identify and quarantine any detected malware or potentially unwanted programs.

App 2: Bitdefender - Comprehensive Security Suite

Bitdefender offers a suite of security tools, including antivirus, firewall, and privacy protection.

Step 1: Installing Bitdefender

Visit the Bitdefender website or download the Bitdefender app from the Mac App Store.

Install the app and create a Bitdefender account.

Step 2: Running Security Scans

Open Bitdefender and perform a full system scan to check for viruses and malware.

Use the app's features to manage your privacy settings and secure online activities.

App 3: NordVPN - Virtual Private Network

NordVPN is a VPN service that encrypts your internet connection and enhances privacy.

Step 1: Subscribing to NordVPN

Visit the NordVPN website and subscribe to a plan that suits your needs.

Download and install the NordVPN app from the website.

Step 2: Using NordVPN

Open NordVPN and log in using your account credentials.

Choose a server location and connect to the VPN to secure your internet connection and maintain privacy.

App 4: LastPass - Password Manager

LastPass helps you manage and secure your passwords for various online accounts.

Step 1: Installing LastPass

Visit the LastPass website or download the LastPass app from the Mac App Store.

Create a LastPass account and set up a master password.

Step 2: Managing Passwords

LastPass will prompt you to save and generate passwords when you log in to websites.

Access your saved passwords and log in automatically using the LastPass browser extension.

Tips:

- Regular Updates: Keep your security apps and operating system updated for optimal protection.
- Safe Browsing: Exercise caution when downloading files or clicking on links to avoid potential threats.

Using Financial and Productivity Trackers

Tracker apps provide valuable tools for organizing your finances and optimizing your productivity.

App 1: Mint - Financial Tracking and Budgeting

Mint is a comprehensive financial tracker that helps you monitor your expenses, set budgets, and track your financial goals.

Step 1: Signing Up for Mint

Visit the Mint website and sign up for a free account.

Connect your bank accounts, credit cards, and other financial accounts to Mint.

Step 2: Managing Finances

Explore your financial dashboard to view your transactions, categorize expenses, and track your income.

Set up budget categories and receive alerts when you approach budget limits.

App 2: YNAB - You Need A Budget

YNAB is a budgeting app that focuses on giving every dollar a purpose and helping you prioritize your spending.

Step 1: Creating a YNAB Account

Visit the YNAB website and sign up for an account.

Set up budget categories based on your spending priorities.

Step 2: Budgeting and Expense Tracking

Allocate funds to specific categories and adjust your budget as needed.

Enter transactions as you spend money and categorize expenses.

App 3: Todoist - Productivity and Task Management

Todoist is a task management app that helps you organize your daily routines and boost productivity.

Step 1: Setting Up Todoist

Visit the Todoist website or download the Todoist app from the Mac App Store.

Sign up for a Todoist account and log in.

Step 2: Managing Tasks

Create tasks and organize them into projects or categories.

Set due dates, priorities, and labels for each task.

App 4: Toggl - Time Tracking and Productivity Analytics

Toggl is a time-tracking app that helps you monitor how you spend your time and identify productivity trends.

Step 1: Registering with Toggl

Visit the Toggl website and sign up for an account.

Download the Toggl app or use the web version.

Step 2: Tracking Time

Create projects and tasks in Toggl to represent your activities.

Start and stop timers to track the time you spend on each task.

Tips:

- Consistency: Make it a habit to update your tracker apps to ensure accurate information regularly.
- Review and Reflect: Review your financial and productivity data to identify trends and make improvements.

Language Learning and Productivity Apps

Language learning apps and productivity tools can work together to help you master a new language effectively.

App 1: Apple Translate - Language Learning Assistant

Apple Translate is a powerful app that helps you learn and practice new languages.

Step 1: Accessing Apple Translate

Open the Apple Translate app pre-installed on your MacBook Air 2023.

Select the source and target languages for translation and learning.

Step 2: Learning and Practicing

Use the Conversation mode to practice speaking and listening in the target language.

Explore the Vocabulary mode to learn new words and phrases.

App 2: Anki - Intelligent Flashcards

Anki is a flashcard app that uses spaced repetition to help you memorize vocabulary and concepts.

Step 1: Installing Anki

Visit the Anki website and download the Anki app for your MacBook Air.

Create an AnkiWeb account to sync your flashcards.

Step 2: Creating and Reviewing Flashcards

Create flashcards with words or phrases in your target language.

Review flashcards daily, and Anki will adapt the review schedule based on your performance.

App 3: Duolingo - Gamified Language Learning

Duolingo offers a gamified approach to language learning, making it engaging and interactive.

Step 1: Signing Up for Duolingo

Visit the Duolingo website or download the Duolingo app from the Mac App Store.

Create a Duolingo account or log in if you have one.

Step 2: Learning Modules and Practice

Now, complete lessons in various modules, including vocabulary, grammar, and listening.

Earn points and track your progress as you learn.

App 4: Focus Booster - Pomodoro Technique for Language Learning

Focus Booster is a productivity app that uses the Pomodoro Technique to enhance focus and retention.

Step 1: Installing Focus Booster

Visit the Focus Booster website and download the app.

Create an account or log in if you have one.

Step 2: Using the Pomodoro Technique

Set a timer for a focused study session (e.g., 25 minutes).

Take short breaks between study sessions to enhance retention.

Tips:

- Consistency: Dedicate regular time to language learning to maintain progress.
- Practice Speaking: Use language learning apps to practice speaking and listening skills.

Using Apple Pay

Apple Pay allows you to make purchases and payments using your MacBook Air 2023, providing a seamless and secure way to transact without sharing your card details.

Step 1: Setting Up Apple Pay

Open "System Preferences" from the Apple menu.

Click on "Wallet & Apple Pay."

Click "Add Card" and follow the instructions to add your credit or debit card to Apple Pay. You can also add cards from your iPhone if they are already set up there.

Step 2: Making Payments with Apple Pay

- Online Payments:

When shopping on a website that supports Apple Pay, select the Apple Pay option during checkout.

Confirm your purchase details and use Touch ID or Face ID to authenticate the payment.

- In-Store Payments:

Look for the Apple Pay logo at contactless payment terminals in stores.

Hover your MacBook Air over the terminal while it's awake and unlocked. Use Touch ID or Face ID to authenticate the payment.

Step 3: Sending and Receiving Money with Apple Pay

Open the "Messages" app on your MacBook Air.

Start or reply to a conversation with the person you want to send money to.

Click the "Apple Pay" icon in the message thread.

Enter the amount you want to send and choose the payment source (if you have multiple cards set up).

Authenticate the payment using Touch ID or Face ID.

Step 4: Managing Apple Pay Cards and Transactions

Open the "Wallet" app on your MacBook Air to view your cards and recent transactions.

Add, remove, or manage cards from the Wallet app settings.

To see recent transactions, click on a card and view the transaction history.

Tips:

- Security: Apple Pay uses tokenization and device-specific numbers to secure your card information.
- Supported Merchants: Look for the Apple Pay logo or contactless payment signs at supported merchants.

- Privacy: Your transactions are private, and merchants do not see your card details.

Using FaceTime

FaceTime allows you to stay connected with friends and family through high-quality video and audio calls, making it easy to communicate, share moments, and collaborate from a distance.

Step 1: Initiating a FaceTime Call

Click on the "FaceTime" app icon in your Applications folder or Dock to open the app.

Sign in with your Apple ID if prompted (or use your MacBook Air's Apple ID).

In the FaceTime app, click the "+" button in the top-right corner.

Enter the name, email address, or phone number of the person you want to call.

Click the "Video" or "Audio" button to start the call.

Step 2: During a FaceTime Call

- During a video call:

Use the camera switch button to toggle between the front and rear cameras.

Mute your microphone by clicking the microphone icon.

Adjust call volume and screen brightness using the on-screen controls.

- During an audio call:

Use the on-screen controls to mute or unmute your microphone.

Adjust call volume using the on-screen commands.

Step 3: Adding and Managing Contacts

Click the "Contacts" tab in the FaceTime app to view your contacts.

Click the "+" button to add new contacts by entering their details.

To manage your contacts, right-click on a contact's name and select "Edit" to update their information.

Step 4: FaceTime Preferences

Click "FaceTime" in the menu bar and select "Preferences."

Customize FaceTime settings, such as your caller ID, blocked contacts, and more.

Step 5: Group FaceTime Calls

To initiate a group FaceTime call, start with one person, then click the "+" button to add more participants.

You can also create a FaceTime call from a group conversation in the "Messages" app.

Using Safari Browser

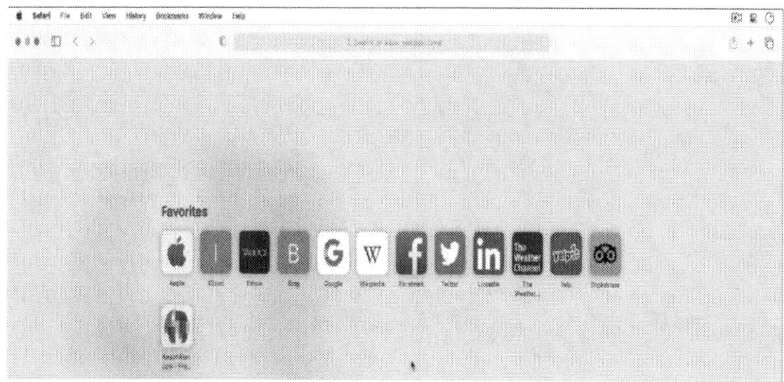

Safari is a powerful and user-friendly browser that allows you to explore the internet, search for information, and interact with websites.

Step 1: Opening Safari and Navigating to a Website

Click the "Safari" app icon in your Applications folder or Dock to open the browser.

In the address bar at the top, type the URL of the website you want to visit (e.g., www.example.com) and press "Enter" or "Return."

Step 2: Tab Management

- Open a New Tab:

Click the "+" button on the right side of the tab bar.

Press "Command" + "T" on your keyboard.

- Switch Between Tabs:

Click on a tab to switch to it.

Use the keyboard shortcuts "Command" + "1" through "9" to switch to specific tabs.

- Close Tabs:

Click the "x" button on the tab you want to close.

Use the keyboard shortcut "Command" + "W."

Step 3: Bookmarks and Favorites

- Adding Bookmarks:

Click "Bookmarks" in the menu bar and select "Add Bookmark."

Please choose a location to save the bookmark and give it a name.

- Accessing Bookmarks:

Click "Bookmarks" in the menu bar to access your bookmarks.

Use the keyboard shortcut "Command" + "Shift" + "B."

- Adding to Favorites:

Click the "Open in Favorites" button (star icon) in the address bar to add the current site to your Favorites.

Step 4: Search and Smart Search Bar

- Searching the Web:

Type your search query in the search bar (address bar) and press "Enter" or "Return."

Safari will display search results from your default search engine.

- Smart Search Bar:

The search bar also acts as an address bar. Type a URL here to navigate directly to a website.

Step 5: Reader View and Reader Preferences

- Reader View:

When available, click the "Reader" button (book icon) in the address bar to view articles in a clean and distraction-free format.

- Reader Preferences:

Customize Reader view by clicking the "AA" button in the address bar.

Adjust font size, background color, and more for a comfortable reading experience.

Tips:

- Extensions and Plugins: Explore Safari extensions and plugins for added functionality.
- Private Browsing: Use private browsing mode without saving history or cookies.
- Gestures: Use trackpad gestures to navigate between tabs and perform actions.

Advanced App Usage Tips

Your MacBook Air is a powerful tool that can be optimized for enhanced app performance and productivity.

Tip 1: Multi-Touch Gestures for App Navigation

- Swipe Between Full-Screen Apps:

Swipe left or right with three or four fingers to switch between full-screen apps.

- Mission Control and App Exposé:

Use a three-finger swipe up to open Mission Control for a bird's-eye view of your open windows.

Swipe down with three fingers to activate App Exposé for a quick view of all windows for a specific app.

Tip 2: Split View and Multitasking

- Split View:

Click and hold an app window's green "Full-Screen" button to enter Split View.

Drag another app's window to the other side to use both apps.

- Picture-in-Picture (PiP) Mode:

While watching a video, click the PiP button to make the video window float on top of other apps.

Tip 3: Custom Keyboard Shortcuts

- Customize Shortcuts:

Open "System Preferences," go to "Keyboard," and click "Shortcuts."

Create custom keyboard shortcuts for app functions you frequently use.

Tip 4: Automator for Workflow Automation

- Automate Tasks:

Open "Automator" from the Applications folder and create workflows to automate repetitive tasks.

- Save and Use Automator Workflows:

Save your workflows as applications and execute them with a simple double-click.

Tip 5: Terminal for Advanced Tasks

- Launch Terminal:

Open "Terminal" from the Utilities folder to access the command-line interface.

- Perform Advanced Actions:

Use the Terminal for file manipulation, system maintenance, and more.

Tip 6: Customizing App Preferences

- Explore App Settings:

Take time to explore the preferences and settings of your apps to tailor them to your needs.

- Sync and Cloud Services:

Configure app preferences to sync data across devices or use cloud services for seamless access.

Tip 7: Accessibility Features for Enhanced Productivity

- VoiceOver:

Enable VoiceOver in the "Accessibility" settings to have your MacBook Air read the text and interface elements aloud.

- Zoom and Magnifier:

Use Zoom and Magnifier settings to enhance visibility and readability.

Tip 8: Spotlight Search for Quick Access

- Keyboard Shortcut:

Use "Command" + "Space" to open Spotlight and quickly find apps, files, and information.

- Calculator and Currency Conversion:

Type math calculations or currency conversions directly into Spotlight.

CHAPTER TEN

Introduction to the Metaverse with MacBook Air 2023

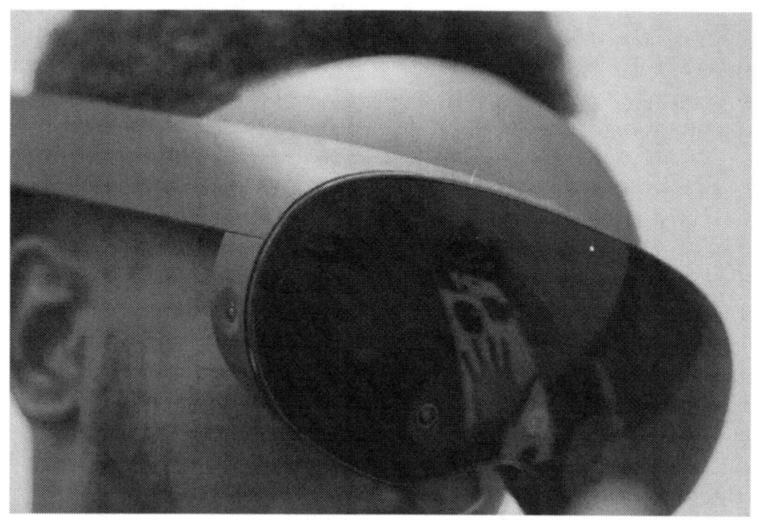

The metaverse is a collective virtual shared space that merges physical and digital realities. It's a vast interconnected network of digital platforms, environments, and experiences. Think of it as a three-dimensional internet, where users can interact with each other and digital objects in real time. It's a convergence of augmented reality (AR), virtual reality (VR), and the internet, creating a seamless blend of the physical and digital worlds.

Here are some vital implications to consider:

- **Enhanced Collaboration and Communication:**

The metaverse opens up new avenues for collaborative work and communication. With your MacBook Air, you can access metaverse platforms to connect with colleagues, friends, or family in shared virtual spaces. Imagine attending virtual meetings, workshops, or social gatherings in immersive 3D environments.

- **Creative Expression and Entertainment:**

Your MacBook Air can serve as a portal to creative expression within the metaverse. Engage with artistic platforms to create, showcase, and share your digital artwork, music, or designs. Additionally, enjoy immersive entertainment experiences like concerts, theater performances, and virtual tourism, all from the comfort of your MacBook Air.

- **Learning and Education:**

For beginners and learners, the metaverse offers exciting educational opportunities. Use your MacBook Air to access educational simulations, virtual classrooms, and interactive learning environments. Explore historical events, scientific concepts, and cultural heritage sites in a new way.

Getting Started with the Metaverse on Your MacBook Air

Now that you understand the metaverse's implications let's explore how to get started using your MacBook Air:

- **Choose Metaverse Platforms:**

Research and choose metaverse platforms compatible with your MacBook Air. Look for those with a user-friendly interface, diverse content, and smooth performance.

- **Install Necessary Software:**

Install any required software or applications on your MacBook Air to access the Metaverse. Follow the platform's installation instructions carefully.

- **Create Your Virtual Identity:**

Many metaverse platforms allow you to create a virtual avatar. Customize your avatar to represent yourself digitally, adding a personal touch to your metaverse experience.

- **Explore and Interact:**

Launch the Metaverse platform on your MacBook Air and start exploring. Visit virtual spaces, attend events, interact with other avatars, and experiment with different features.

- **Stay Safe and Mindful:**

While navigating the metaverse, prioritize your online safety. Be cautious about sharing personal information and follow platform guidelines.

Remember that the metaverse, like the internet, requires responsible and respectful behavior.

Metaverse Platforms and Applications

These platforms offer a range of immersive experiences, from social interactions to creative expression and education.

- Decentraland

Platform Overview: Decentraland is a virtual world powered by blockchain technology. Users can create, own, and monetize content and applications within this decentralized metaverse.

Compatibility: Decentraland is accessible through web browsers, making it compatible with your MacBook Air.

Features and Uses:

Create and customize your own virtual spaces, known as "LAND."

Participate in social events, art exhibitions, and virtual gatherings.

Buy, sell, and trade virtual assets using blockchain-based tokens.

- VRChat

Platform Overview: VRChat is a social platform that enables users to create and share their 3D avatars and environments. It focuses on user-generated content and social interactions.

Compatibility: VRChat can be used on your MacBook Air via the web browser or by downloading the macOS client.

Features and Uses:

Interact with users from around the world in immersive 3D environments.

Create and customize your avatars and worlds without programming knowledge.

Attend virtual parties, events, and conferences hosted by the VRChat community.

- Mozilla Hubs

Platform Overview: Mozilla Hubs is a web-based platform for creating and sharing virtual spaces. It's designed for easy collaboration and communication.

Compatibility: You can access Mozilla Hubs directly through web browsers on your MacBook Air.

Features and Uses:

Create private or public virtual rooms for meetings, workshops, or social gatherings.

Customize environments using simple tools and 3D models.

Collaborate with others in real-time, with options for voice and text chat.

- AltspaceVR

Platform Overview: AltspaceVR is a social VR platform that hosts various events and activities, including comedy shows, meetups, and workshops.

Compatibility: AltspaceVR offers a macOS client, allowing you to enjoy the platform on your MacBook Air.

Features and Uses:

Attend live events, performances, and discussions in virtual reality.

Connect with people based on shared interests and hobbies.

Create your events or spaces for personal or professional purposes.

- Rec Room

Platform Overview: Rec Room is a creative and social platform offering games, experiences, and interactive spaces.

Compatibility: Rec Room is accessible on your MacBook Air through web browsers or by downloading the macOS client.

Features and Uses:

Engage in various activities, from playing games to creating art and experiences.

Join user-generated games, events, and challenges.

Collaborate with others to build interactive spaces using intuitive creation tools.

Virtual Reality (VR) and Augmented Reality (AR) Support

While MacBook Air 2023 doesn't natively support high-end VR experiences like those powered by dedicated VR gaming systems, it can still provide access to specific VR applications and experiences. Here's how:

Web-Based VR: Some VR experiences and applications can be accessed through web browsers on your MacBook Air. These experiences are usually less resource-intensive and offer a glimpse into the world of VR.

VR Video and Content: Use your MacBook Air to watch VR videos and explore 360-degree content on platforms like YouTube or Vimeo.

Simple VR Applications: Some lightweight VR applications and games designed for less powerful hardware can be enjoyed on your MacBook Air.

- AR Compatibility on MacBook Air:

Augmented Reality brings digital elements into the real world. While the MacBook Air doesn't have built-in AR capabilities, you can still engage with AR using your laptop:

Mobile AR Apps: Connect your MacBook Air to an iOS device (like an iPhone or iPad) that supports ARKit. Run AR apps on your mobile device and experience augmented reality elements with your laptop.

AR Content Creation: Use AR creation tools on your MacBook Air to design interactive and engaging AR experiences for compatible devices.

- External Hardware and Accessories:

If you're eager to explore more robust VR experiences, consider external hardware and accessories that can enhance your MacBook Air's capabilities:

External GPU: Connect an external graphics processing unit (GPU) to your MacBook Air to enable more demanding VR applications.

VR Headsets: Some VR headsets offer compatibility with MacBook Air through HDMI or USB-C connections, enabling more immersive VR experiences.

AR Glasses: Keep an eye on emerging AR glasses that could offer seamless AR experiences when paired with your MacBook Air.

- Software and Applications:

To fully leverage VR and AR technologies, explore software and applications that cater to your MacBook Air's capabilities:

Web-Based VR Platforms: Discover VR experiences accessible through web browsers, allowing you to explore virtual spaces and content.

AR Apps: Use AR apps on your mobile device that interact with your MacBook Air to blend digital elements into your physical surroundings.

Content Creation Tools: Engage with VR and AR content creation tools enabling you to design, develop, and share your immersive experiences.

Virtual Meetings and Collaboration

Step 1: Choosing a Metaverse Platform

Select a metaverse platform with virtual meeting, and collaboration features compatible with your MacBook Air. Platforms like Decentraland, VRChat,

Mozilla Hubs, and AltspaceVR offer diverse environments for hosting virtual gatherings.

Step 2: Accessing the Metaverse

Open your chosen Metaverse platform through a web browser on your MacBook Air or by installing any necessary applications. Sign in or create an account to start exploring.

Step 3: Hosting or Joining Virtual Meetings

Step 3.1: Hosting a Meeting:

Create a virtual space within the metaverse platform, customizing it according to your preferences.

Set up seating arrangements, presentation screens, and interactive elements within your virtual space.

Invite participants by sharing a link or code to your virtual meeting room.

Step 3.2: Joining a Meeting:

Receive an invitation or link from the meeting host.

Click on the link or enter the provided code to enter the virtual meeting space.

Customize your avatar to represent yourself and interact with others.

Step 4: Collaboration Tools in the Metaverse

Step 4.1: Shared Whiteboards and Screens:

Many metaverse platforms offer collaborative brainstorming, presentations, and idea-sharing tools.

Utilize shared whiteboards or screens to draw, write, and display content for all participants.

Step 4.2: Real-Time Interactions:

Engage in natural conversations through voice and text chat, mirroring real-life interactions.

Use gestures, emotes, and non-verbal cues to enhance communication.

Step 4.3: Interactive Activities:

Plan interactive activities such as icebreakers, team-building exercises, or workshops within the virtual environment.

Collaborate on creative projects using virtual art tools or design software available within the metaverse.

Step 5: Etiquette and Best Practices

Step 5.1: Respect Personal Space:

Be mindful of personal boundaries and respectful of other participants' space.

Avoid intrusive actions that may disrupt the meeting experience.

Step 5.2: Dress Appropriately:

Choose an avatar appearance and attire suitable for the meeting or collaboration.

Professional attire may be preferred for formal business discussions.

Step 5.3: Maintain Engagement:

Stay actively engaged during virtual meetings, just as in physical meetings.

Contribute to discussions, ask questions, and participate in group activities.

Virtual Commerce and Marketplace

Virtual commerce involves buying and selling digital assets, services, or experiences within the metaverse. Metaverse marketplaces are online platforms where users can list, discover, and engage in virtual items, land, art, and more transactions.

Step 1: Choosing a Metaverse Marketplace

Select a Metaverse marketplace compatible with your MacBook Air. Popular options include Decentraland Marketplace, OpenSea, Rarible, and SuperRare. Research each platform's features, fees, and community to find the best fit for your needs.

Step 2: Accessing a Metaverse Marketplace

Access your chosen marketplace through a web browser on your MacBook Air. Sign up or log in to create an account and begin exploring listings.

Step 3: Engaging in Virtual Commerce

Step 3.1: Buying Virtual Assets:

Browse listings for digital art, collectibles, virtual real estate, and more.

Click on an item to view detailed information, images, and seller details.

Use the provided options to purchase the item using cryptocurrency or other supported payment methods.

Step 3.2: Selling Virtual Assets:

List your digital assets by uploading images, descriptions, and relevant details.

Set a price and choose whether the item is available for instant purchase or through auction.

Manage your listings and respond to inquiries from potential buyers.

Step 3.3: Trading and Bartering:

Some marketplaces allow users to trade virtual assets directly or participate in auctions.

Engage in negotiations or propose trades with other users to exchange value items.

Step 4: Virtual Commerce Tips and Best Practices

Step 4.1: Research and Verify:

Research sellers and listings before purchasing to ensure credibility and authenticity.

Verify the legitimacy of digital assets and virtual properties before engaging in transactions.

Step 4.2: Understand Fees and Policies:

Familiarize yourself with the marketplace's fees, transaction costs, and terms of use.

Be aware of any platform-specific guidelines for buying, selling, or trading.

Step 4.3: Secure Your Transactions:

Use secure payment methods and wallets when making purchases or receiving payments.

Be cautious when sharing personal or financial information, and avoid potential scams.

Creating and Customizing Avatars

Step 1: Choosing a Metaverse Platform

Select a Metaverse platform that supports avatar creation and customization, compatible with your MacBook Air. Platforms like VRChat, Decentraland, and AltspaceVR offer avatar customization tools.

Step 2: Accessing the Avatar Customization Tools

Log in to your chosen Metaverse platform through a web browser on your MacBook Air or by downloading any necessary applications.

Step 3: Creating Your Avatar

Step 3.1: Select a Base Avatar:

Choose a base avatar that serves as the foundation for your customization.

Some platforms provide pre-made avatars that you can start with.

Step 3.2: Personalizing Features:

Customize facial features, skin tone, eye color, hairstyle, and other physical attributes.

Adjust details like eyebrows, facial hair, and makeup to match your desired look.

Step 3.3: Wardrobe and Accessories:

Browse through the available clothing and accessory options to find your style.

Mix and match clothing items, shoes, hats, and glasses.

Step 3.4: Animation and Gestures:

Some platforms allow you to customize your avatar's animations and gestures.

Choose expressions, poses, and movements that reflect your personality.

Step 4: Fine-Tuning and Previewing

Use the preview feature to see your avatar's appearance in different poses and environments. Make adjustments until you're satisfied with your avatar's appearance.

Step 5: Name and Identity

Select a virtual name or username for your avatar that resonates with your digital identity within the metaverse.

Step 6: Saving and Using Your Avatar

Step 6.1: Save Your Avatar:

Once content with your avatar's look, save your customizations within the Metaverse platform.

Step 6.2: Importing to Other Platforms:

Some platforms allow you to export or import your avatar across different metaverse platforms.

Step 7: Best Practices

Step 7.1: Be Unique and Creative:

Experiment with different customization options to create a truly unique avatar.

Reflect on your real-life personality or explore new personas.

Step 7.2: Consider Platform Guidelines:

Be aware of any platform-specific guidelines or restrictions regarding avatar customization.

Ensure your avatar complies with the platform's terms of use.

Step 7.3: Have Fun and Express Yourself:

Avatar customization is an opportunity for self-expression and creativity.

Enjoy the process of bringing your digital persona to life.

CHAPTER ELEVEN

Privacy and Security Considerations

Step 1: Understand Privacy Risks

- Data Collection:

Recognize that metaverse platforms may collect data about your interactions, preferences, and behaviors.

Understand how your data is used and shared by reviewing the platform's privacy policy.

- Identity Exposure:

Be cautious about sharing personal information that could lead to the identification of your real-life identity.

Use virtual personas and avatars to maintain a degree of separation between your digital and physical selves.

Step 2: Secure Your Account

- Strong Passwords:

Create strong, unique passwords for your Metaverse platform accounts.

Use letters, numbers, symbols, and uppercase/lowercase characters.

- Two-Factor Authentication (2FA):

Enable 2FA for an extra layer of security.

Receive a verification code on your mobile device when logging in to your account.

Step 3: Protect Your Device

- Update Software:

Regularly update your MacBook Air's operating system and applications to ensure you have the latest security patches.

- Antivirus Software:

Install reputable antivirus software to detect and prevent potential threats.

- Use Trusted Networks:

Connect to secure and trusted Wi-Fi networks to reduce the risk of unauthorized access.

Step 4: Manage Permissions

- App Permissions:

Review and manage permissions granted to metaverse applications on your MacBook Air.

Limit access to sensitive data and features whenever possible.

- Privacy Settings:

Adjust privacy settings within metaverse platforms to control who can see your activities and interactions.

Step 5: Be Cautious with Sharing

- Personal Information:

Be selective about sharing personal information in virtual conversations or interactions.

Avoid sharing sensitive details like your home address or financial information.

- Screenshots and Recordings:

Be aware that others may take screenshots or record interactions within the metaverse.

Think twice before sharing content that you wouldn't want to be public.

Step 6: Educate Yourself

- Stay Informed:

Keep up-to-date with the latest privacy and security developments within the metaverse.

- Verify Platforms:

Verify its legitimacy and reputation before using a metaverse platform to avoid scams.

Metaverse Accessibility Features

By considering the diverse needs of all participants, you can contribute to a more welcoming and inclusive metaverse experience.

Step 1: Why Accessibility Matters

Accessibility ensures that all users, regardless of physical or cognitive abilities, can fully engage with the metaverse.

Inclusivity promotes equal opportunities for participation, interaction, and collaboration.

- Common Accessibility Needs:

Visual impairments: Consider users with low vision or blindness who may require screen readers or high contrast settings.

Hearing impairments: Think about users who are deaf or hard of hearing and may need captions or visual cues.

Motor impairments: Keep in mind users with limited mobility who may require alternative input methods.

Step 2: MacBook Air Accessibility Options

- VoiceOver:

Enable VoiceOver on your MacBook Air to provide spoken descriptions of on-screen elements.

VoiceOver assists users with visual impairments in navigating and interacting with metaverse platforms.

- Zoom and Magnifier:

Utilize Zoom and Magnifier features to enlarge on-screen text, images, and content; this benefits low-vision users, making it easier to read and interact within the metaverse.

- Captions and Subtitles:

Enable captions and subtitles for video and audio content within Metaverse applications; this supports users with hearing impairments by providing a visual representation of spoken content.

- Accessibility Shortcuts:

Customize accessibility shortcuts to toggle between different accessibility features on your MacBook Air quickly.

Step 3: Metaverse Accessibility Considerations

- Platform Features:

Choose metaverse platforms that prioritize accessibility and offer features like text-to-speech and closed captions.

- Text and UI Elements:

Ensure that text and user interface elements within virtual spaces are legible and in high contrast.

- Gestures and Controls:

Provide alternative gestures and controls to accommodate users with limited dexterity.

- Spatial Audio:

Implement spatial audio cues to help users with visual impairments navigate virtual environments.

Step 4: Inclusive Virtual Interactions

- Communicate Clearly:

Use clear and concise language in virtual conversations, events, and activities.

- Gesture Descriptions:

Offer descriptions of meaningful gestures or actions that are taking place within virtual spaces.

- Collaborative Tools:

Choose metaverse tools that allow collaborative interactions, accommodating different communication preferences.

Step 5: Continuous Learning and Improvement

Stay informed about the latest accessibility guidelines and best practices for the metaverse.

Regularly update your MacBook Air's accessibility settings based on your needs.

Metaverse for Education and Learning

As technology transforms our learning, the metaverse offers innovative and immersive opportunities to expand your educational horizons.

Step 1: The Metaverse's Role in Education

- Virtual Learning Environments:

The metaverse provides interactive and engaging virtual learning spaces, fostering active participation and collaboration.

- Exploration and Immersion:

Explore historical events, scientific concepts, and cultural sites in three-dimensional, immersive environments.

- Hands-On Learning:

Engage in simulations, experiments, and practical exercises within virtual spaces.

Step 2: Choosing Educational Metaverse Platforms

- Decentraland:

Explore Decentraland's virtual museums, galleries, and educational simulations.

- VRChat:

Attend virtual lectures, workshops, and interactive learning sessions within VRChat.

- Mozilla Hubs:

Create virtual classrooms, conduct group discussions, and host lectures on Mozilla Hubs.

- AltspaceVR:

Participate in educational events, debates, and discussions hosted by the AltspaceVR community.

Step 3: Utilizing Metaverse for Learning

- Virtual Field Trips:

Take students on virtual field trips to historical landmarks, museums, and scientific simulations.

- Immersive Simulations:

Simulate complex concepts like chemistry reactions, physics experiments, and ecological systems.

- Collaborative Projects:

Collaborate on group projects, presentations, and workshops within virtual classrooms.

- Guest Speakers and Experts:

Invite guest speakers and experts worldwide to conduct virtual lectures and Q&A sessions.

Step 4: Accessibility and Inclusivity

- Accessibility Features:

Ensure metaverse platforms offer accessibility features like closed captions and voice-to-text options.

- Diverse Learning Styles:

Accommodate diverse learning styles by incorporating visual, auditory, and kinesthetic elements.

- Inclusive Interactions:

Foster inclusive interactions by using metaverse tools that support multiple communication modes.

Step 5: Evaluating Learning Outcomes

Assess student engagement, participation, and understanding of concepts within the metaverse environment.

Step 6: Privacy and Safety

Implement privacy measures and follow security guidelines to protect students' information and well-being.

Metaverse Health and Wellness

The metaverse offers unique opportunities to prioritize your mental and physical health, from relaxation to physical activity.

Step 1: The Metaverse's Role in Health and Wellness

- Mindfulness and Meditation:

Use metaverse platforms to access guided meditation sessions and mindfulness exercises.

Create serene virtual environments to unwind and practice relaxation techniques.

- Fitness and Physical Activity:

Use virtual workouts, yoga classes, and dance sessions within metaverse platforms.

Track your physical activity and set fitness goals to stay motivated.

- Social Connection and Support:

Join virtual wellness communities, support groups, and discussion forums to connect with like-minded individuals.

Attend virtual wellness events and workshops to foster social connections.

Step 2: Metaverse Wellness Platforms

- VR Wellness Apps:

Explore VR applications dedicated to guided meditation, relaxation, and stress reduction.

- Fitness Metaverse Platforms:

Discover platforms that offer virtual fitness classes, workouts, and challenges.

- Virtual Retreats and Events:

Participate in metaverse wellness retreats and events focused on self-care and personal development.

Step 3: Creating Your Wellness Spaces

- Virtual Yoga Studios:

Design virtual yoga studios within metaverse platforms to practice yoga and stretching.

- Serene Meditation Gardens:

Create calming virtual gardens where you can meditate and practice mindfulness.

- Dance and Exercise Zones:

Set up virtual spaces for dance sessions, cardio workouts, and exercise routines.

Step 4: Mind-Body Connection

- Biofeedback Integration:

Explore platforms that integrate biofeedback devices to monitor and enhance your wellness practices.

- Visualization Techniques:

Utilize metaverse tools for immersive visualization exercises that promote relaxation and positivity.

Step 5: Balancing Screen Time

Be mindful of screen time and take breaks to rest your eyes and stretch your body.

Step 6: Privacy and Well-being

Prioritize your well-being by setting boundaries and taking breaks to prevent digital fatigue.

Step 7: Virtual Nature Exploration

Immerse yourself in virtual natural environments to experience the calming effects of nature.

Metaverse Development and Coding

Your MacBook Air 2023 is your window into the world of coding, enabling you to build and shape the metaverse according to your imagination.

Step 1: Learning Programming Languages

- Python:

Python is beginner-friendly and versatile, making it an excellent choice for metaverse development.

- JavaScript:

JavaScript is essential for web-based metaverse platforms and interactive experiences.

- C#:

C# is widely used for creating experiences within platforms like VRChat and Unity.

Step 2: Metaverse Development Tools

- Unity:

Unity is a powerful engine for creating 2D, 3D, and VR/AR experiences within the metaverse.

- Unreal Engine:

Unreal Engine offers tools for designing high-quality interactive experiences and virtual environments.

- A-Frame:

A-Frame is a web framework for building virtual reality experiences that work directly in web browsers.

- Decentraland SDK:

The Decentraland SDK allows you to create, own, and monetize content within the Decentraland metaverse.

Step 3: Online Coding Resources

- Codecademy:

Codecademy offers interactive coding lessons for various programming languages.

- Coursera:

Coursera provides online courses on metaverse development, game design, and programming.

- Udemy:

Udemy offers various courses on Unity, Unreal Engine, and coding for the metaverse.

- YouTube Tutorials:

Explore YouTube for video tutorials on metaverse development, coding techniques, and platform-specific guides.

Step 4: Metaverse Communities and Forums

- Stack Overflow:

Stack Overflow is a valuable resource for getting answers to coding-related questions.

- Reddit Communities:

Subreddits like r/metaverse and r/gamedev offer platforms for discussions, sharing ideas, and seeking advice.

- Discord Servers:

Join Discord servers dedicated to metaverse development, where you can connect with like-minded enthusiasts.

Step 5: Practice and Projects

- Build Small Projects:

Start with small coding projects to practice your skills and gain confidence.

- Metaverse Experiments:

Experiment with creating basic virtual environments, interactions, and assets within metaverse platforms.

- Collaborative Projects:

Join open-source metaverse projects or collaborate with others to enhance your skills.

Managing Metaverse Accounts

Whether you're an avid explorer of different metaverse platforms or a content creator with various identities, mastering the art of account management ensures seamless navigation and organization.

Step 1: Account Creation and Organization

- Separate Email Addresses:

Consider using a different email address for your Metaverse account to keep them distinct from your email.

- Password Management:

Use a reliable password manager to store and manage your login credentials for each account securely.

- Username Consistency:

Maintain a consistent username or handle across different metaverse platforms for easy identification.

Step 2: Browser Profiles and Bookmarks

- Browser Profiles:

Create separate browser profiles for each Metaverse account to keep your logins separate.

- Bookmarks and Favorites:

Organize your metaverse-related bookmarks and favorites within each browser profile.

Step 3: Multi-Account Support

- Platform Features:

Some metaverse platforms offer built-in multi-account support, allowing you to switch between accounts easily.

- Extensions and Add-ons:

Explore browser extensions or add-ons that enable quick switching between different accounts.

Step 4: Incognito/Private Browsing

- Incognito Mode:

Use the incognito/private browsing mode to temporarily log in to a different Metaverse account without affecting your main session.

- Temporary Sessions:

Keep a separate incognito/private browsing window for each Metaverse account you manage.

Step 5: Desktop Applications

- Platform-Specific Apps:

Some metaverse platforms offer standalone desktop applications with multi-account support.

- Multiple Instances:

Consider running multiple instances of platform applications; each logged in to a different account.

Step 6: Clearing Cookies and Data

- Log Out:

Always log out of your Metaverse accounts when you're finished using them.

- Clear Cookies and Cache:

Periodically clear your browser's cookies and cache to ensure a fresh session when switching accounts.

Step 7: Security Considerations

- Secure Your Device:

Ensure your MacBook Air 2023 is protected with strong passwords, biometric authentication, and encryption.

- Account Recovery:

Familiarize yourself with each platform's account recovery process to regain access.

- Two-Factor Authentication (2FA):

Enable 2FA for additional security on your Metaverse accounts.

Metaverse Experience Optimization

Here are instructions to optimize your laptop settings, enabling you to seamlessly navigate virtual environments, engage in immersive experiences, and connect with others across the metaverse.

Step 1: Update macOS for Peak Performance

Keeping your macOS up to date is crucial for optimal performance. Follow these steps:

Click on the Apple logo in the top-left corner of the screen.

Select "System Preferences."

Choose "Software Update."

If updates are available, click "Update Now."

Step 2: Manage Energy Saver Settings

Efficient energy usage can prolong battery life and boost performance during metaverse adventures:

Go to "System Preferences."

Select "Energy Saver."

Adjust "Turn display off after" and "Put hard disks to sleep when possible" to suitable durations.

Enable "Slightly dim the display while on battery power."

Step 3: Optimize Graphics Performance

Enhance visual quality and responsiveness for metaverse experiences:

Navigate to "System Preferences."

Choose "Energy Saver."

Click on the "Graphics" tab.

Select "Higher performance" to optimize graphics quality.

Step 4: Clear Storage and Optimize Disk Performance

A clutter-free disk improves overall system speed:

Open "About This Mac" from the Apple menu.

Go to the "Storage" tab.

Click on "Manage" to remove unnecessary files.

Use the "Optimize" button to improve disk performance.

Step 5: Adjust Trackpad and Mouse Settings

Fine-tune navigation controls for comfortable metaverse exploration:

Visit "System Preferences."

Choose "Trackpad" or "Mouse."

Adjust tracking speed and scrolling options according to your preference.

Step 6: Maximize Internet Connection

Smooth metaverse interactions rely on a stable internet connection:

Click the Wi-Fi icon in the menu bar.

Select "Open Network Preferences."

Choose "Advanced."

Reorder your preferred networks to prioritize the fastest ones.

Step 7: Enable the "Do Not Disturb" Mode

Minimize interruptions during metaverse sessions:

Click the Notification Center icon in the top-right corner.

Enable "Do Not Disturb" mode.

Step 8: Update Metaverse Applications

Ensure metaverse apps are up to date for compatibility and performance improvements:

Open the App Store.

Click on "Updates."

Update metaverse-related applications.

Future Trends and Integration

The metaverse is rapidly evolving, opening up exciting possibilities for integrating advanced technologies with devices like the MacBook Air 2023. Here, we'll see some emerging trends and potential integrations that could reshape how we interact with the metaverse using our laptops and other cutting-edge technologies.

- Emerging Trends:

1. Virtual Reality (VR) and Augmented Reality (AR) Integration

We can expect deeper integration with the MacBook Air as VR and AR technologies advance. Imagine donning lightweight VR glasses that seamlessly connect to your laptop, allowing you to step into immersive virtual environments easily. This integration could enhance gaming experiences, virtual collaboration, and educational simulations.

2. Haptic Feedback and Sensory Immersion

Future MacBook Air iterations might incorporate haptic feedback mechanisms, enabling users to feel sensations and textures within the metaverse; this would further blur the line between the physical and digital worlds, making interactions more lifelike and engaging.

3. AI-Powered Personalization

Artificial Intelligence could be pivotal in tailoring metaverse experiences to individual users. Your MacBook Air could analyze your preferences, behaviors, and interactions to curate personalized virtual environments and content that resonate with you.

4. Cross-Platform Metaverse Interaction

The metaverse could become a cross-platform ecosystem where MacBook Air users seamlessly interact with users on other devices, such as smartphones, VR headsets, and smart glasses. This integration would foster a more inclusive and interconnected metaverse experience.

- Potential Integrations:

1. Metaverse-Compatible Processor and Graphics Enhancements

Future MacBook Air models might have specialized processors and graphics cards optimized for metaverse applications; this would ensure smooth performance, realistic visuals, and efficient multitasking while navigating complex virtual spaces.

2. Metaverse-Enhanced Productivity Tools

Imagine a metaverse-integrated version of productivity software where you can collaborate with colleagues, attend virtual meetings, and manipulate data in a shared virtual workspace using your MacBook Air. This integration could revolutionize remote work and collaborative projects.

3. Metaverse Social Networking

MacBook Air could seamlessly integrate with metaverse-based social platforms, allowing you to interact with friends, family, and colleagues in virtual spaces. You might attend virtual events, share experiences, and build connections in ways that go beyond traditional social media.

4. Wearable Metaverse Accessories

Innovative wearables, such as high-tech gloves or wristbands, could complement the MacBook Air's capabilities by providing tactile feedback, gesture recognition, and enhanced interaction within the metaverse. These accessories could amplify the sense of immersion and control.

CHAPTER TWELVE

Introduction to AI on MacBook Air

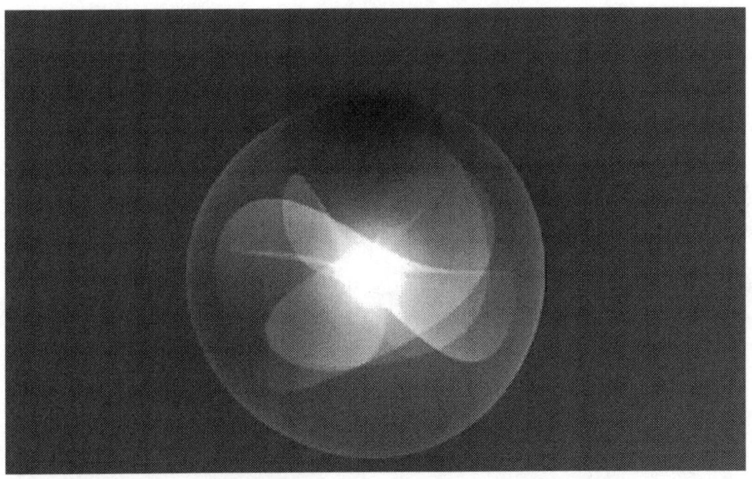

AI, or Artificial Intelligence, refers to the simulation of human intelligence in machines that can perform tasks that typically require human intelligence. On your MacBook Air 2023, AI is integrated into various applications and functionalities, enhancing your user experience. These AI-driven features include:

Siri: Your intelligent virtual assistant, Siri, is powered by AI. It can help you with tasks, answer questions, set reminders, send messages, and more. Click the Siri icon in the menu bar or use the "Hey Siri" voice command to activate Siri.

Spotlight Search: Spotlight uses AI to search your MacBook Air for files quickly and accurately, applications, documents, and even web results. Press Command + Space to open Spotlight and start typing your search query.

Photo and Video Enhancements: AI technology enhances images and videos by improving lighting, color balance, and quality. When you open the Photos app, you'll notice AI-driven suggestions for editing and organizing your media.

- Using AI-Powered Applications

Now that you have a basic understanding of AI on your MacBook Air let's explore how you can use AI-powered applications effectively:

Photos: Open the Photos app and select a photo. Click the "Edit" button to see AI-powered suggestions for enhancing your image. Experiment with different tips to see the improvements.

Mail: When composing an email, AI can assist you by offering predictive text suggestions. As you type, these suggestions will appear above the keyboard. Tap on them to quickly complete sentences.

Siri Assistant

Siri, your AI virtual assistant, is a powerful tool to help you with various tasks and queries. To start using Siri on your MacBook Air 2023, follow these steps:

Click the Siri Icon: Look for the colorful icon in your menu bar's top-right corner. It resembles a multicolored sound wave. Click on it to activate Siri.

Voice Activation (Optional): If you prefer hands-free operation, you can enable voice activation for Siri. Open "System Preferences" from the Apple menu, select "Siri," and check the box next to "Listen for 'Hey Siri.'"

Step 1: Basic Tasks and Queries

Siri is designed to assist you with a variety of tasks and questions. Here are some everyday tasks you can perform using Siri:

a) Opening Apps and Files:

Say, "Open [app name]" or "Open [file name]." For example, "Open Safari" or "Open Document.txt."

b) Sending Messages and Making Calls:

To send a message, say, "Send a message to [contact's name]," and dictate your message. Siri will confirm before doing it.

For making calls, say, "Call [contact's name]." Siri will initiate the call for you.

Step 2: Asking Questions and Getting Information

Siri can provide you with answers to general knowledge questions and information. Here's how:

a) General Queries:

Ask questions like, "What's the weather today?" or "How tall is the Eiffel Tower?"

b) Math and Conversions:

Try saying, "What's 20% of 150?" or "Convert 10 miles to kilometers."

c) Language Translation:

You can ask Siri to translate phrases into different languages. For example, "Translate 'hello' to French."

Step 3: Setting Reminders and Alarms

Siri is excellent at helping you manage your schedule:

- Setting Reminders:

Say, "Remind me to [task] [time/day]." For instance, "Remind me to call John at 3 PM."

- Creating Alarms:

Command Siri with, "Set an alarm for [time]." For example, "Set an alarm for 7 AM."

Step 4: System and Device Control

Siri can assist you in controlling various aspects of your MacBook Air:

- Adjusting Settings:

Tell Siri, "Turn on [setting name]," such as "Turn on Bluetooth" or "Turn on Do Not Disturb."

- System Information:

Ask, "What's my battery percentage?" or "How much free space do I have on my disk?"

Step 5: Siri Suggestions

Siri proactively offers suggestions based on your usage patterns. For example:

Siri might suggest playing your favorite playlist if you often listen to music at a specific time.

Step 6: Troubleshooting and Tips

Improve Recognition:

If Siri doesn't understand you correctly, you can correct it by saying, "That's not what I said."

- Feedback:

To help Siri understand you better, provide feedback on Siri's responses. Say, "That's not helpful," or "You got that wrong."

Voice Dictation and Transcription

Step 1: Enabling Voice Dictation:

Voice dictation allows you to speak naturally and have your words converted into text. To enable this feature:

Click on the Apple menu in the top-left corner of your screen.

Select "System Preferences."

Choose "Keyboard" from the options.

Navigate to the "Dictation" tab.

Toggle the "Dictation" option to turn it on.

Choose your preferred language from the drop-down menu.

Click "Enable Dictation."

Step 2: Using Voice Dictation:

Now that voice dictation is enabled, follow these steps to use it effectively:

Open any text field or document where you want to insert text.

Press the "fn" (function) key twice on your keyboard. A microphone icon will appear.

Start speaking clearly and naturally. Your spoken words will be converted into text in real time.

Once you're done talking, press the "fn" key again to stop dictation.

Tips:

Speak at a moderate pace and pause slightly between sentences for accurate transcription.

Punctuation can be inserted by saying commands like "period," "comma," "question mark," etc.

Step 3: Transcribing Audio Files:

The transcription feature allows you to convert pre-recorded audio files into text. Here's how:

Open the "TextEdit" application on your MacBook Air.

Create a new document or open an existing one.

Click "Edit" in the menu bar and select "Start Dictation."

Open the audio file you want to transcribe in another media player or application.

Listen to the audio and speak the content into your MacBook's microphone.

The transcribed text will appear in the TextEdit document as you say.

Tips:

Ensure your microphone is correctly set up, and there's minimal background noise for accurate transcription.

Use headphones with a built-in microphone for better audio quality during transcription.

Step 4: Editing and Formatting:

After the voice dictation or transcription, you might need to edit and format the text:

Highlight the transcribed text.

Use standard keyboard shortcuts (e.g., Command + B for bold, Command + I for italics) or the format options in your application to apply formatting.

Edit errors or inaccuracies manually by clicking on the text and making changes.

Step 5: Saving and Sharing:

Once you have transcribed or dictated the text, save and share it as needed:

Click "File" in the menu bar.

Select "Save" or "Save As" to save the document.

Choose your desired file format (e.g., .docx, .pdf).

Select the destination folder and click "Save."

AI-Enhanced Photo Editing

Step 1: Opening the Photo in Preview

To get started with AI-powered photo editing, follow these steps:

Locate the photo you wish to edit on your MacBook Air 2023.

Right-click on the picture, select "Open With," then choose "Preview."

Step 2: Auto-Enhance with AI

The AI-powered Auto-Enhance feature automatically improves various aspects of your photo. Here's how to use it:

With the photo open in Preview, click on the "Markup" icon (which looks like a toolbox) in the toolbar.

Select the "Adjust Color" button.

Click "Auto Levels" to automatically adjust the photo's brightness, contrast, and color balance.

Step 3: Removing Imperfections with AI

You can easily remove imperfections from your photo using AI-powered tools:

Click the "Markup" icon again and select "Adjust Color."

Choose the "Retouch" option.

Adjust the brush size using the slider on the right.

Click and drag over imperfections, blemishes, or unwanted objects to remove them seamlessly.

Step 4: Enhancing Specific Elements

Use AI-powered tools to enhance specific elements in your photo:

Click on the "Markup" icon and select "Adjust Color."

Choose "Smart Lasso."

Draw a rough outline around the element you want to enhance (e.g., a person's face).

Select from various enhancement options, such as "Lighten," "Darken," "Sharpen," or "Define."

Adjust the intensity of the enhancement using the slider.

Step 5: AI-Powered Filters and Effects

Apply creative filters and effects to your photo using AI:

Click on the "Markup" icon and select "Adjust Color."

Choose the "Filters" option.

Explore the various AI-generated filters available.

Click on a filter to apply it to your photo. Adjust the filter's strength using the slider.

Step 6: Saving Your Edited Photo

Once you are satisfied with your AI-enhanced edits, save the photo:

Click on "File" in the menu bar.

Select "Export."

Choose your desired format (e.g., JPEG) and quality.

Select the destination folder and click "Save."

AI-Based Search and Spotlight

Step 1: Accessing Spotlight

Spotlight is a powerful tool for searching for files, applications, and information on your MacBook Air. To use it:

Press the "Command" (⌘) and "Space" keys simultaneously, or click on the magnifying glass icon in the top-right corner of the menu bar.

Step 2: Conducting a Basic Search

Spotlight can quickly find files and applications based on keywords. Here's how:

In the Spotlight search bar, type keywords related to the file, application, or information you seek.

As you type, Spotlight will provide instant results, including files, applications, documents, and more.

Step 3: Utilizing AI-Powered Suggestions

Spotlight provides AI-generated suggestions to enhance your search experience:

Start typing a keyword in the Spotlight search bar.

Observe the suggested results, including documents, websites, and news.

Click on a suggestion to access the related content directly.

Step 4: Extending Search Beyond Files

Spotlight can go beyond files and applications to provide quick access to additional information:

Search for unit conversions, currency conversions, and mathematical calculations directly in the Spotlight search bar.

Type "Weather" followed by a location to instantly get the weather forecast.

Enter "Define" followed by a word to receive its definition.

Step 5: Preparing Quick Calculations

You can use Spotlight as a calculator for basic math:

Open Spotlight by pressing the "Command" (⌘) and "Space" keys.

Type a mathematical expression (e.g., 25 * 4) in the Spotlight search bar.

Press "Enter" to see the calculated result.

Step 6: Launching Applications and Files

Spotlight makes launching applications and opening files a breeze:

Open Spotlight using the keyboard shortcut or the magnifying glass icon.

Start typing the name of the application or file you want to open.

Spotlight will display matching results. Click on the desired application or file to launch it.

Step 7: Customizing Spotlight Preferences

Tailor Spotlight to your preferences and needs:

Go to "System Preferences" from the Apple menu.

Select "Spotlight."

Customize search categories (e.g., Applications, Documents, Messages) by checking or unchecking the boxes.

Arrange the order of search categories by dragging and dropping them.

Smart Suggestions and Predictive Typing

Step 1: Enabling Predictive Typing

Predictive typing uses AI to suggest words and phrases as you type. To enable it:

Click on the Apple menu in the top-left corner of your screen.

Select "System Preferences."

Choose "Keyboard" from the options.

Navigate to the "Text" tab.

Check the box next to "Predictive" to enable predictive typing.

Step 2: Using Smart Suggestions

As you type, macOS provides contextually relevant suggestions that can save time and effort. Here's how to use them:

Open any application where you can write, such as Messages or Notes.

Start typing a sentence or phrase.

Observe the grayed-out suggestions that appear above the keyboard.

Press the "Space" key to accept a recommendation, and the suggested word or phrase will be completed.

Step 3: Accepting Corrections and Suggestions

Smart suggestions not only include words but also offer corrections. Follow these steps to accept hints and corrections:

Type a word that macOS suggests correcting.

The proposed edit will appear in the suggestion bar.

To get the improvement, press the "Right Arrow" key or click on the suggestion in the bar.

Step 4: Customizing Smart Suggestions

You can personalize smart suggestions to suit your writing style and vocabulary:

Open "System Preferences" and select "Keyboard."

Go to the "Text" tab.

Click the "+" button to add custom text replacements or shortcuts.

Type a shortcut (e.g., "omw" for "On my way") and the full text it represents.

Click "Done" to save your customizations.

Step 5: Learning from User Behavior

MacBook Air's AI system learns from your typing patterns and adapts over time:

Continue using smart suggestions and predictive typing in various applications.

The AI system observes your typing behavior and refines suggestions based on your usage.

Step 6: Multilingual Support

MacBook Air's smart suggestions and predictive typing support multiple languages:

Switch your keyboard language by clicking on the language icon in the menu bar.

Start typing in the selected language, and the AI will adapt to provide relevant suggestions.

Step 7: Correcting Mistakes

In the rare event of incorrect suggestions, use these steps to correct errors:

Type the word correctly without accepting the hint.

The AI will learn from this correction and adapt future recommendations.

AI in Video and Audio Editing

Step 1: AI-Powered Video Enhancements

Modern video editing applications leverage AI to enhance visual quality and streamline the editing process:

Open your preferred video editing application on your MacBook Air.

Import the video footage you want to edit.

Look for AI-powered features such as "Auto Color Correction" or "Auto Stabilization."

Apply these features to adjust color balance and brightness and stabilize shaky footage automatically.

Step 2: Facial Recognition and Tracking

AI can automatically detect faces and objects within videos:

Access the video editing application's AI-driven features.

Use "Facial Recognition" or "Object Tracking" tools.

These features help track and follow specific elements within the video, keeping them in focus and enhancing visual storytelling.

Step 3: AI-Powered Audio Enhancements

AI is also used to enhance audio quality and remove background noise:

Launch your audio editing application on your MacBook Air.

Import the audio clip you want to edit.

Explore AI features like "Auto Noise Reduction" or "Voice Enhancement."

Apply these features to eliminate unwanted background noise and enhance vocal clarity.

Step 4: Automatic Transcription

Some AI-powered applications can transcribe audio to text:

Find an audio editing tool with automatic transcription capabilities.

Import the audio file you want to transcribe.

Initiate the transcription feature, and the AI will convert spoken words into text, simplifying content creation and editing.

Step 5: Music and Soundtrack Suggestions

AI can offer suggestions for music and sound effects:

Look for AI-integrated audio editing software.

Explore the "Music Suggestions" or "Soundtrack Generator" feature.

The AI will analyze your audio content and suggest appropriate background music or sound effects to enhance the mood.

Step 6: AI-Powered Rendering and Export

AI streamlines the rendering and exporting process:

Finalize your video or audio edits.

Choose the export option within your editing application.

Some AI-enhanced tools optimize settings for various platforms (e.g., social media) to ensure optimal playback quality.

Step 7: Staying Updated

AI-driven advancements in video and audio editing continue to evolve:

Stay informed about software updates for your chosen editing applications.

Manufacturers often introduce new AI-powered features, so regularly check for updates to access the latest enhancements.

AI-Driven Virtual Assistants in Apps

Step 1: Integration of AI-Powered Virtual Assistants

Many third-party apps on your MacBook Air 2023 incorporate AI-driven virtual assistants to offer enhanced functionality:

Open any supported third-party app (e.g., productivity, communication, or task management).

Look for the presence of a virtual assistant, often indicated by a microphone icon, chat bubble, or similar symbol.

Step 2: Personalized Task Management

AI-powered virtual assistants help manage tasks within apps:

Open a task management app that integrates a virtual assistant.

Use natural language to create, edit, or prioritize tasks.

The virtual assistant processes your commands, making task management more intuitive and efficient.

Step 3: Conversational Interactions

Virtual assistants engage in natural language conversations within apps:

Access a supported messaging or communication app.

Initiate a conversation with the virtual assistant using text or voice commands.

Ask questions, request information, or perform actions directly within the app's interface.

Step 4: Enhanced Information Retrieval

Virtual assistants retrieve information from within apps using AI:

Open an app that integrates a virtual assistant for information retrieval (e.g., a news or research app).

Ask the virtual assistant for specific topics, articles, or data.

The virtual assistant provides relevant information from within the app's content.

Step 5: Seamless Integration with Siri

Some third-party apps offer Siri integration for voice-based interactions:

Access the Siri icon or voice command ("Hey Siri").

Ask Siri to perform tasks or retrieve information within the supported third-party app.

Step 6: Continuous Learning and Adaptation

AI-driven virtual assistants improve over time through user interactions:

Regularly engage with the virtual assistant within supported apps.

The AI system learns from your preferences and behavior, providing increasingly accurate and relevant assistance.

Step 7: Privacy and Data Security

Understand the privacy measures in place for AI-driven virtual assistants within apps:

Data processing often occurs locally on your MacBook Air, minimizing external data transfers.

Review app permissions and privacy settings to ensure your interactions remain secure and confidential.

CHAPTER THIRTEEN

AI for Data Analysis and Insights

Step 1: Install and Set Up AI-driven Application for Data Analysis

Begin by installing a user-friendly AI-driven application suitable for data analysis. We recommend "Tableau Public," a powerful tool offering intuitive drag-and-drop data visualization and analysis features.

Visit the Tableau Public website (https://public.tableau.com/en-us/s/gallery) using your MacBook Air's web browser.

Download and install the Tableau Public application.

Launch the application and create a free account if prompted.

Step 2: Import and Prepare Data for Analysis

Now that you have the AI tool ready, it's time to import and prepare your data for analysis.

Locate your dataset (e.g., CSV, Excel) and ensure it is properly organized and formatted.

Open Tableau Public and click on the "Connect to Data" option.

Select your data source and follow the on-screen instructions to import the data.

Step 3: Utilize AI Tools for Data Analysis and Insights

With your data imported, let's use AI-driven features to analyze and gain insights.

Drag and drop relevant data fields onto the workspace to create a visualization canvas.

Explore the "Show Me" feature, which automatically suggests suitable chart types based on your data.

Experiment with AI-powered forecasting: right-click on a data point and choose "Forecast" to predict future trends.

Step 4: Visualize and Interpret Results

Now that you have insights, it's time to visualize and interpret them for a better understanding.

Customize your visualizations: click and drag to modify axes, labels, colors, and titles.

Use filters and parameters to explore different aspects of your data interactively.

Add annotations and descriptions to highlight key findings and trends.

Tips:

- Save your project regularly to avoid data loss.
- Utilize online tutorials and forums to learn advanced features of Tableau Public.
- Stay curious and explore different chart types to find the best representation for your data.

AI-Enhanced Security

AI-powered security measures use algorithms to analyze patterns, detect anomalies, and make decisions in real-time.

Step 1: Exploring Facial Recognition Technology

Facial recognition is a biometric technology that identifies or verifies individuals based on their unique facial features. It's used for secure access control and user authentication.

Open "System Preferences" on your MacBook Air.

Click "Security & Privacy" and then the "Privacy" tab.

Select "Camera" on the left panel and ensure that the app you want to use facial recognition with has access to the camera.

Step 2: Using Face ID for Biometric Authentication

Face ID is an advanced form of biometric authentication that uses facial recognition technology to unlock your MacBook Air and authenticate transactions.

Go to "System Preferences" and navigate to "Security & Privacy."

Click on the "General" tab and enable "Use Face ID" to unlock your MacBook Air.

Follow the prompts to set up Face ID by positioning your face within the frame.

Enjoy seamless and secure access to your device using Face ID.

Step 3: Utilizing AI-Enhanced Security Features

MacBook Air 2023 uses AI-enhanced security measures to protect your device and data.

Open "System Preferences" and go to "Security & Privacy."

Click on the "General" tab and enable "FileVault" to encrypt your data.

Enable "Find My" to track your MacBook Air in case of loss.

Tips:

- Keep your facial recognition data and biometric information secure.
- Regularly update your MacBook Air's software for the latest security enhancements.
- Enable two-factor authentication for added security.

AI in Calendar and Scheduling

Step 1: Enable Calendar Suggestions

AI in your MacBook Air 2023 can provide intelligent suggestions for scheduling events based on your routines and habits. To enable this feature:

Open the "Calendar" app from your MacBook Air's dock or Applications folder.

Click on the "Calendar" menu in the top left corner and choose "Preferences."

Navigate to the "General" tab and check the box next to "Show time suggestions."

Close the preferences window.

Step 2: Creating Smart Events

AI can help you create events more efficiently by understanding natural language input. Here's how:

In the "Calendar" app, click on your event's desired date and time slot.

In the event details window, type a natural language description of the event. For example, "Meet with John for lunch on Friday at 12:30 PM."

The AI will automatically detect the event details and populate the relevant fields as you type.

Review the details, add the necessary information, and click "Add" to create the event.

Step 3: Optimizing Travel Time

Let AI assist you in calculating travel time between events to avoid scheduling conflicts:

Create a new event or edit an existing one.

Enter the event location and enable "Location" by clicking the "Add Location" button.

AI will estimate travel time based on traffic conditions and your preferred transportation mode.

Adjust the event start and end times to account for travel time automatically suggested by AI.

Step 4: Rescheduling with AI Insights

If you need to reschedule an event, AI can provide insights into the best available time slots:

Click on the event you want to reschedule.

Choose "Reschedule" from the options.

AI will analyze your calendar and suggest optimal time slots based on availability and preferences.

Select a suggested time, manually adjust as needed, and confirm the change.

Step 5: Handling Conflicts

AI can help you manage scheduling conflicts effortlessly:

AI will notify you when a scheduling conflict arises and provide alternative options.

Click on the conflict notification to see available solutions.

Review the suggested options and choose the one that works best for you.

The conflicting event will be automatically rescheduled to the new time slot.

Using AI in Creative Design

Whether you're a graphic designer, illustrator, or simply someone who loves to create, incorporating AI into your workflow can open new doors of creativity.

Step 1: AI-Generated Art

Transform your photos into unique works of art with AI-generated styles:

Visit the "App Store" on your MacBook Air and search for AI-powered art apps.

Download and install a preferred app (e.g., Prisma) with AI-generated art styles.

Open the app, select a photo, and apply various artistic filters inspired by famous artists or styles.

Experiment with different filters until you achieve the desired artistic effect.

Step 2: AI-Assisted Vector Illustration

Create intricate vector illustrations with AI assistance:

Launch your preferred vector illustration software (e.g., Adobe Illustrator).

Draw a rough outline of your design using the pen or brush tool.

Activate the AI-powered "Auto Trace" feature to refine your sketch into precise vector lines.

Edit and enhance the vector paths as needed to achieve your desired design.

Step 3: AI-Enhanced Typography

Elevate your typography game with AI-driven text design:

Open a design software (e.g., Adobe Photoshop) on your MacBook Air.

Create a new document and add a text layer with your desired text.

Explore the AI-powered text effects or styles available in the software.

Adjust font, color, and spacing parameters to customize the AI-generated text design.

Step 4: AI-Based Color Palette Generation

Let AI suggest harmonious color palettes for your designs:

Use a web-based color palette generator with AI algorithms (e.g., Colormind).

Upload an image or describe your design concept to the AI tool.

Receive AI-generated color palette suggestions based on the input provided.

Apply the suggested color palette to your design for a visually appealing result.

AI-Based System Maintenance

Step 1: Automatic Performance Optimization

AI can help keep your MacBook Air in top shape by automatically optimizing performance. Here's how:

Open "System Preferences" from the Apple menu or the dock.

Click on "Energy Saver" and enable "Automatic graphics switching" to allow the system to manage GPU usage efficiently.

Navigate to "Displays" and ensure "Automatically adjust brightness" is selected for energy-efficient screen brightness management.

Step 2: AI-Enhanced Storage Management

AI can intelligently manage your storage to free up space and enhance performance:

Go to the Apple menu and select "About This Mac."

Click on the "Storage" tab to view your storage usage.

Click on "Manage" to open the Storage Management tool.

Let AI analyze your storage and suggest ways to optimize it, such as deleting large and unused files.

Step 3: AI-Powered Battery Management

AI can help extend your MacBook Air's battery life and health:

Open "System Preferences" and select "Energy Saver."

Enable "Battery" settings like "Put hard disks to sleep when possible" and "Slightly dim the display while on battery power."

Click on the battery icon in the menu bar to view battery usage details and AI suggestions for battery life extension.

Step 4: Proactive Troubleshooting with AI

AI can identify and address potential issues before they impact your MacBook Air's performance:

Launch "Applications" and open "Console."

Explore the logs and error messages to identify any recurring issues.

If available, use Apple's AI-driven "Diagnostics & Usage Data" feature to send diagnostic information for analysis and potential solutions automatically.

Future of AI on MacBook Air

Here are some emerging trends and possibilities that could shape how AI is integrated into future MacBook Air models, enhancing user experiences and opening new avenues of innovation.

- Trends:

Enhanced Personalization: Future MacBook Air models could offer even more personalized experiences by using AI to adapt to individual user preferences, behaviors, and work patterns; this could include tailoring user interfaces, suggesting relevant applications, and predicting user needs.

Advanced Voice Interfaces: With the rise of natural language processing and voice recognition, future MacBook Airs could feature advanced voice interfaces that allow users to interact with their devices more naturally and efficiently; this could involve voice-controlled commands for various tasks, such as navigating the operating system and executing commands within applications.

Proactive Assistance: AI could evolve to offer proactive assistance by anticipating user actions and needs. Imagine your MacBook Air suggesting optimal times to schedule tasks, reminding you of important events, and even offering solutions to potential issues before they arise.

Deeper Integration with Creative Workflows: For users engaged in creative endeavors, future MacBook Airs could leverage AI to enhance creative workflows; this might involve AI-driven content creation tools, intelligent image and video editing assistance, and even AI-generated design recommendations.

More innovative Battery Management: AI could significantly extend battery life and optimize power consumption. Future MacBook Air models might use AI to manage background processes intelligently, adjust performance based on usage patterns, and provide real-time battery life predictions.

- Possibilities for AI Integration:

AI-Powered Multitasking: Future MacBook Airs could intelligently manage multitasking by predicting which applications you'll likely use and allocating system resources accordingly, leading to smoother multitasking experiences.

AI-Enhanced Security: AI could enhance security features, such as advanced facial recognition, behavior-based authentication, and real-time threat detection, to safeguard user data.

Emotional Intelligence: As AI progresses, future MacBook Air models might incorporate expressive intelligence features, such as recognizing and responding to user emotions, leading to more empathetic interactions.

Environmental Impact Monitoring: AI could help track and manage the environmental impact of your device usage, offering insights and suggestions for reducing energy consumption and carbon footprint.

CONCLUSION

Our exploration discovered the MacBook Air 2023 lightweight design, which effortlessly combines portability with performance. We've navigated the user-friendly interface, mastering essential skills like setting up your device, browsing the web, and effortlessly managing files. Along the way, we've highlighted the power of multitasking, security measures, and connectivity options, ensuring you're well-equipped to make the most of your MacBook Air.

The MacBook Air 2023 is not merely a tool; it's an enabler of dreams. As you go aboard on your tech journey, remember that every click, swipe, and keystroke brings you closer to realizing your aspirations. Stay curious, explore fearlessly, and let your MacBook Air be your companion on this exciting adventure. Your knowledge of this noteworthy device is just the beginning—your potential knows no bounds.

ABOUT THE AUTHOR

Curtis Campbell is an intelligent and innovative computer scientist with experience in software engineering. As a renowned technology expert, his passion for capturing still photos and motion pictures has led him into photography and videography, which he is doing with excellence. Curtis has produced several tutorials on different topics. As a researcher and a prolific writer with proficiency in handling tech products, he learned different approaches to managing issues on the internet and other applications.

Made in United States
Troutdale, OR
04/11/2024